How To Be Smart Parents

Now That Your Kids Are Adults

Sylvia Auerbach

Silvercat Publications
San Diego, California

10 9 8 7 6 5 4 3 2 1

Library of Congress Cataloging-in-Publication Data

Auerbach, Sylvia.
    How to be smart parents : now that your kids are adults /
Sylvia Auerbach.
        p.   cm.
    ISBN 0-9624945-8-5 : $14.95
    1. Parent and adult child.   I. Title
HQ755.86.A94   1995
306.874—dc20   94-37659
                                                    CIP

Printed in the United States of America

Dedication

To my husband and best friend, Albert, three great parents, sons Carl and Steven and daughter-in-law Pamela, and my six delightful grandchildren, the two Davids, and Josh, Miriam, Ben, and Laura

This is a very wise and warm "guidebook" about family pain and family healing. It covers all the important sources of tension and confusion that beset grown children and their parents. It is a pleasure to read—jargon free, direct, and good-humored.

Kenneth Kressel, Ph.D.
Professor of Psychology
Rutgers University

OTHER BOOKS BY SYLVIA AUERBACH

An Insider's Guide to Auctions

A Woman's Guide To Managing Money

A Woman's Book of Money

Your Money: How to Make It Stretch

Table of Contents

About the Author

Sylvia Auerbach graduated from the University of Pennsylvania and received advanced degrees from Columbia University School of Journalism and the London School of Economics. She is the author of four other books: An Insider's Guide To Auctions; A Woman's Guide To Managing Money: A Woman's Book Of Money; *and* Your Money: How To Make It Stretch. *She has written articles for numerous magazines and newspapers, including* Changing Times; Cosmopolitan; The New York Times; Real Estate Review; *and* Sunday's Woman.

Sylvia is a member of the Writers' Guild and the American Society of Journalists and Authors. She has taught feature writing at a number of major American universities, including Temple, St. Johns (NY), City College of New York, Barnard, and the New School for Social Research. From 1987 to 1990, she directed the Book Publishing Institute of the University of Pennsylvania. She has also been an Associate Editor at Publishers Weekly *and Managing Editor at* Library Journal. *In addition, she has been a consultant to Merrill Lynch and the R. R. Bowker Company.*

She received the Helen Slade Sanders Fellowship to Columbia University School of Journalism and the Faculty Fellowship Achievement Award of the Geriatric Education Center of Pennsylvania.

Sylvia lives near Philadelphia with her husband Albert. She is the mother of two sons and the grandmother of six grandchildren.

Introduction

Welcome to the world of middle-age parenting.

Like other stages in parenting, it has its delights, its dilemmas—and its dreams. Here's a dream many of my friends and I have shared:

> *Our adult children think we're the greatest and compare us favorably to other people's parents, who aren't nearly as close to perfect as we are. They don't blame us for any of their childhood traumas, all of which were the fault of the times or were caused by outsiders, not us. As they reached adulthood, they always consulted with us and asked our advice. If their lives haven't turned out quite they way they expected, they don't hold us responsible.*
>
> *They approve of how we mothers color our hair and use make-up. They approve of how we fathers dress. They call us frequently and remember our birthdays and anniversaries.*
>
> *They think we're wonderful grandparents. They're convinced we know more about parenting than they do. Everything we do for, and with, their children is exactly right.*
>
> *If by chance we made some minor mistakes as they were growing up, they have forgiven us many times over.*

Now hit the snooze button and slip into another dream, the one our adult children dream about us.

> *We never mention past mistakes they have made, give them unsolicited advice, or suggest solutions to their problems.*

We think they made the best possible choices of spouses or lovers. We approve of their lifestyle, we are impressed by how well they manage their finances, and we admire their house-keeping skills.

We never ask them when they are going to make us grand-parents. If they already have children, we never question the way they are raising them. We think they are doing a won-derful job, especially in the way they enforce discipline and teach manners.

We don't mind at all if they choose to go somewhere else on holidays. We never expect them to call or visit on a regu-lar schedule. We never make them feel guilty by reminding them of anything we've done for them.

Now the alarm goes off. Wake up and smell the coffee, the real world of middle-age parenting. How the times have changed since we were the adult children of *our* parents!

We couldn't wait to finish college, leave our parent's nest, and get out on our own. Our children stretch out their college years and face a poor job market, hesitating to leave home or rushing to move back in. We worried about becoming old maids or not being able to support a wife and family. They wonder whether they should get married at all. We hardly knew divorce. They count it among their friends and acquaintances. We had *His* and *Hers* towels. They have *His* and *Hers* children.

It is a different world, for sure. Yet one fact of life hasn't changed. Like parents from time immemorial, we haven't stopped being parents. We're still parts of our children's lives, in good times and bad, sharing the pleasures and helping soothe the pain. And something else is new: unlike our parents, we are going to share twenty, thirty, or even forty years with our adult children. That makes it all the more important that these be good years.

This can be a challenge. We have no script to guide us through this longer-lasting changed world. We can't always follow the path of our parents. Like them, for example, we value and want respect, but we can't simply revert back to their authoritarian ways of demanding it—*We are your parents...that's why.* Nor do we accept the beliefs so many of them held that the parent-child generation gap is too wide to build a bridge across or that we can't understand or empathize with the younger generation.

Still, in this age of communication, how many of us wonder why we find it difficult to communicate with our adult children? This is not to say that families today, compared with families of the past, have more than ordinary difficulty with their "interpersonal adjustments," to use the current popular-psychology jargon (which we ordinary folks would call "getting along with the kids"). In true American fashion, we believe that when there are problems, there are solutions. If there are no one-size-fits-all solutions, then there must be a solution that fits us.

Certainly, we ought to be able to do more than just cope. Yet that is what many of us are doing. Isn't there something that we could have, would have, or should have done differently? Was there a better way? And why should each of us have to reinvent the parental wheel on our own? After all, the psychologists, psychotherapists, social workers, demographers, and academics studying and treating today's families have lots of valuable information available to them. Why shouldn't it be available to everyone as well?

Hence, this book. The professionals I interviewed had much experience dealing with families which were in trouble, but their knowledge was valuable for all families. Not that they had all the answers. It was something of a relief for me to learn that even these experts were themselves parents who, in addition to their studies and research, had learned from the mistakes they'd made with their own children.

The more research I did, the more experts I interviewed, the more reflection I gave to my own life, the more I came to appreciate that what really counts in life is the family. And the more I realized that, like all things in life, if you want something valuable—and what could be more valuable than a strong, caring family?—you have to plan for it, work at it, and accept that you'll never reach perfection, but that it really doesn't matter. What does matter is the learning and enjoyment you experience along the way, taking the strikeouts with the home runs and helping your children, grandchildren, and yourself achieve your potential as a loving family.

I regret that I can't list the many professional organizations which have helped me in the research for this book, but I am very grateful to them. I am also indebted to the academic, clinical, and private-practice psychologists, sociologists, financial planners, and university professors who have graciously shared their expertise with me.

I thank my husband, Albert, who never begrudged the shared time we gave up while I wrote this book. I am grateful to my son, Dr. Carl Auerbach, a psychotherapist and professor of psychology, who was always available for a hasty phone consultation, and to my good friend and excellent lawyer, Murray Richmond. I own special thanks to two friends: Edward Schultz, who got me started writing this book, and Dr. Sayre Schatz, who spurred me on.

I own lots of thank-yous to the many parents who gave generously of their time to tell me how they got along with their children, what they did poorly or well, and what they would love to do over again. I learned from them as well as from the experts.

I enjoyed writing this book. I hope you find it as worthwhile and rewarding to read as I found it to write.

CHAPTER I

Who Is The Family?

*When Nancy exchanged "I do's" with her second hus-
band, his three small daughters were at the ceremony. So was
Sue, one of her best friends and also her former mother-in-
law. Sue had baked a huge cake for the reception. Nancy's
first husband sent flowers.*

*Cheryl's colleagues gave her a surprise shower when, after
seven years of living together, she and Paul finally set a wedding date. All four parents came to the shower, relieved that
the couple had finally decided to abide by their religion and
get married.*

*When Patricia accepted Joe's proposal of marriage, she
knew his three-year-old daughter, the child of his affair with
a divorcée, would live with them. The child had been his responsibility since her mother left Joe and the court awarded
him custody.*

Welcome to the New World of Marriage and the Family

For those of us who gave birth to the babyboomers, the world
of our children can be a strange place. We used to take the
answers for granted when we talked about what marriage
was and who were family members. Now, these have become
mind-boggling questions. We often may feel like an endangered species, the last representatives of what may be the last
era of the traditional family.

Arlene Skolnick, a research psychologist at the University of California, Berkeley, has spent much of her professional career studying the American family. She points out that while we grew up with one concept of the family and family values, our family lives today either don't fit this concept at all or, at best, they don't fit it very well.

Most of us, for example, are still married to our original husbands or wives, usually someone from the same religion, the same ethnic background, and often, though we didn't plan it, from the same general neighborhood. Most of us chose to have at least one but typically two or more children, all of whom are now adults.

How different are the families of our adult children! Many of them have mixed (and sometimes mixed-up) marriages. Presbyterians marry Episcopalians, Christians marry Jews, Lutherans marry Catholics. Blacks and whites marry browns and yellows. Northerners marry Southerners. The rodeo marries the garment district. The most interesting wedding I have seen was the union of an Italian-Jewish bride to an English-Polish groom. Grandmom was the caterer, and everyone got happily exhausted dancing Israeli horas, Italian tarantellas, Polish polkas, and English country dances!

Some of these marriages are first marriages, still going strong. There are also divorces, second and even third remarriages. There are lesbian and gay couples and single children still unattached. Many of our children's families have no more than one child, and some are childless by choice. Some have one and only one child, while still others include children from first and second marriages. And this doesn't even exhaust my own circle of friends!

Ask any of these young people who is their family and you'll get a range of answers.

Of course we know who our families are. Or do we? If we actually posed the question to our spouses, our sisters, or our brothers, we might be surprised at the repsonses we would get. We'd probably get as many answers as there are definitions of the family.

Consider the boundaries of a family, for example. Where do we draw the line between 'family' and 'not-family'? Do we mean our immediate family, the so-called nuclear family of spouse and children and no more? Or do we mean the extended family of other kinfolk, and how extended is that extension? Of course, we would include grandchildren. But should we also include uncles, aunts, assorted cousins, and all their children, both those we love and those we really cannot abide? Must we include that brat who locked himself in the second-floor bathroom until the fire department came to get him out?

Or how about the in-laws on both sides? Are they parts of our families? Can we draw the line at the impossible ones, those brothers- and sisters-in law whom we can barely tolerate and by whom the affection is reciprocated? Perhaps we could narrow the family down to blood lines, but even then, at what point do blood ties become too thin to be counted?

The answer used to be simpler. For those of us in the older generation, family usually starts with the nuclear family, plus grandchildren. Then we add the extended family, and we vary how far we protract that extension depending on our blood ties, our old loyalties, and our ethnic heritages.

For better or worse, though, new definitions of family in these changing times have come to include step-families, single parent families, foster families, adoptive families, gay snd lesbian families, etc. In 1992, to illustrate, Massachusetts Mutual Life Insurance Company completed a survey to find out how people defined the word family. Twenty-seven percent said a family was "a group of people related by blood, marriage, or adoption." But sixty-eight percent chose a broader definition: "a group who love and care for each other."

The Family Circle

Sociologists use a much broader and much more flexible definition of the family. The family is a shifting circle, and who is considered within that family circle will vary according to the person, the context, and the timing of the question. Some people may choose a narrow definition: my spouse, my children, my brothers and sisters. Other might add aunts, uncles, cousins…or ignore them altogether. Still others would include close friends or neighbors. All, it turns out, are equally valid conceptions of the family.

We shouldn't be too surprised if our children's families turn out different from our expectations. Ask them *who is in your family?* Their answers may include not only blood ties, but also whom they are living with at the moment, whom they were living with before, whom they are married to now, or whom they were married to previously. Does this confuse us, with our time-tested definitions and maybe still-current opinions? You bet. How could it be otherwise?

If only we could draw the circle the sociologists talk about and make the family as inclusive or exclusive as we wish. We could party with the distant relatives whom we recently met and who've turned out to be really delightful while we black out the phone numbers of the cousin who picks his teeth at the table, the aunt who always asks if we've gained weight, and the uncle who tells gross, dirty jokes. I could even include the cousins I met only once, at a funeral, now that I've learned that their son is a big star in Hollywood!

Wouldn't it be wonderful to be able to stretch or shrink the circle as time goes by? We could force the family, once and for all, to fit our expectations.

If Life Were Only That Simple

In real life, we can't draw this family circle. We're going to have to live with the luck of the draw. And, like it or not, the people in this circle are family, and we will have share with them some kind of relationship, responsibility, and commitment.

The good news is that the circle encompasses people we love, who are as committed to us as we are committed to them. The bad news is that we're not automatically endowed with the wisdom that guarantees we'll understand, let along get along with, everyone in our family; our children's circles overlap ours, not always with the best of results; and family relationships are in a state of flux. We're living under that ancient, apocryphal curse *may you be born in interesting times,* and nothing has prepared us for these changes.

Is it any wonder that we're sometimes, indeed often, confused and ambivalent? It's as if we were given a set of building blocks and a sample of what we could build with them, only to discover that our blocks were a different shape from those in the sample. Parenting has never been easy, but in the past at least we had the advantage of knowing what our roles were. We learned them as children by observing our parents, and we practiced them by playing house. If one playmate said, "You be the mommy," or "You be the daddy," we didn't need a script writer. We knew exactly how to act.

If we are confused, what must it be like for our children? Imagine their children playing house. Consider the possibilities:

⟡ *Both mommy and daddy pick up their make-believe brief-cases and say hello to the babysitter.*

⟡ *The single mommy drops baby off at grandmom's, the day-care center, or the baby sitter's house on her way to make-believe work.*

⟡ *Daddy says goodbye to mommy as she goes off to work and he sets out to change baby's diaper.*

And maybe mommy says goodbye to daddy as he goes off to work while she stays home with the children (and makes ready the defense of her choice in a world which increasingly expects women to be employed outside their homes).

The New American Family

The 1990 Census shows a far different world than the one we grew up in. There are still some traditional families—married couples with young children. According to the Census

Bureau, these were only about twenty-five percent of married couples, down from about forty percent in 1970. For the first time, married couples without children (twenty-eight percent) were more numerous than married couples with children (twenty-seven percent). This trend seems to be continuing. The percentage of married couples with children is falling faster than the percentage of married couples without. If you are looking forward to the day when you hear the words, 'grandma' and 'grandpa,' you may be disappointed.

The Stepfamily Association of America, Inc. points out that "fifty percent of all marriages today are remarriages for at least one person, and of these, sadly, about 60 percent will end in divorce." These remarried couples become the stepfamilies sometimes thought of as 'deficient' families. Most stepmothers and stepfathers do not deserve the poor image they have inherited from the fairy tales we read as children. They need to be considered as legitimate, not deficient, parents, and we can certainly help them by accepting them into the family. (We'll discuss this later in Chapters III and IV.) This is just as true for homosexual couples.

According to the 1990 Census, single parents are the fastest-growing family classification, now constituting about twenty-nine percent of all families with children under eighteen. About eighty-six percent of these are headed by mothers, down from ninety percent in 1970. Only about fourteen percent of these families are headed by single fathers, but this percentage is up from ten percent in 1970.

The shift in living arrangements has been so dramatic that in 1990, for the first time in the history of the United States, the Census Bureau allowed two adults living together as lovers, whether heterosexual or same-sex, to classify themselves as a couple, not as roommates. The Bureau, ever discreet, calls these cohabiting couples 'spousal equivalents.' Those who study families are more likely to refer to these pairings as 'domestic partnerships.' Perhaps a more human-scale term might be 'coupledom.'

These changes have found acknowledgement in public policy as well. Professor Steven K. Wisensale and graduate student Kathlyn E. Heckart point out, in their Domestic Partnerships survey, that fourteen communities, nine corporations, and a number of private organizations already grant these new families some of the benefits that formerly were available only to traditional families. Sooner or later, government employees will undoubtedly receive the same benefits.

Before granting these benefits, some communities require that individuals in domestic partnerships register and complete affidavits on the status of their partnerships. Affidavits may include, among others, such sworn statements as: "Occupant A and Occupant B reside together as a non-married cohabiting couple and intend to do so indefinitely"; "We are not married to anyone"; or "We are each other's sole domestic partner and intend to remain so indefinitely and are responsible for our common welfare." The parties must also register if and when their relationship ends.

Some of us have agonized with a heartbroken daughter involved with a married man or with a disillusioned son whose 'significant other' promised fidelity and then broke the promise frequently and flagrantly. How we wish they could have required such affidavits from their lovers!

What's Behind These Changes?

We can attribute many of these changes to technology and its sometimes unexpected results. As one example, consider that the so-called sexual revolution of the 60s was made possible by a scientific advance: the pill. The pill gave women more control of their sex lives and the choice of sex without fear of pregnancy. As a result, according to some in the feminist movement, any woman could be anything she wanted to be. Have you ever mourned that you were born several decades too soon? That may only be partially true, but the fact remains that the pill was at least as responsible as anything else for rewriting the history of the family.

Another major change was in the economy. Lifetime employment, and the stability it promised, followed the path blazed by the waffle iron and the dance band. Once an icon of middle-class life, job security was one of the casualties of the mass firings within the middle class and the poor job market for new college graduates. It was replaced by an uncertain future and an understandable fear of financial commitments like marriage and children. Add to this the permanence of women with very young children in the work force, some by choice or expectation and many more out of necessity. Many of our kids' families need two incomes to maintain a middle-class standard of living—and sometimes just to survive.

And consider the mixed blessing of increased mobility. Now, hundreds or thousands of miles apart, we stay in touch via the phone and the car, and less frequently via the airplane, the family visit, or the shared vacation. As our actual visits become less frequent, we become more like guests in each others' homes. These carefully planned occasions lack the intimacy that developed when Mom and Dad or Grandmom and Grandpop lived chose by, when visits were frequent and casual, and when families knew each others' joys and problems. Family ties have had to become weaker.

Remember those comic strips where the wife got mad and threatened to go home to mother? Many actually did make the trip, because mother lived nearby. This opportunity to blow off steam may have held some marriages together, to the relief and benefit of many.

Finally, we are seeing new attitudes toward divorce, which is no longer condemned but quite accepted. Colette Dowling, a journalist, mother, and stepmother, traced these new family relationships to changes which began during the 1960s. Her use of the term 'modern serial monogamy' to describe the new carousel of marriage-and-divorce and remarriage-and-divorce is quite fitting.

Because of the high divorce rate and the rise of coupledom instead of marriage, our sons and daughters have to think about their families differently. If they are in long-term relationships, their 'significant others' or 'spousal equivalents' are parts of their families as long as the relationships last. By law, this can't be called a 'common-law' marriage. Perhaps 'common-love' marriage would be an accurate description.

Acceptance and Validation, Not Necessarily Approval

We need to recognize that there is more than one kind of family. Some families are permanent. Others are temporary. All are subject to pressures we never faced. Our reactions to these new arrangements may touch all of our emotions. The joy, surprise, and delight we can handle. But what about the regret, anger, or despair? We have to learn all over again how to deal with these emotions and any ensuing problems which arise. This learning may entail settling old conflicts which may never have been fully resolved before. Most importantly, we have to learn to live with all these new family members if we want to hold on to those we love.

This doesn't mean that we have to love unquestioningly. There is certainly a difference between loving someone and accepting someone. Nor are all of us able to approve of our children's choices in life, whether they pertain to lovers, sexual preferences, or spouses. But we must make it clear to our children that we still love them, even if we can only acquiesce to their choices.

This may be difficult. It is simpler to establish a good relationship with people with whom you share similar backgrounds, interests, and tastes. When you acquire new family members through coupledom, marriage, or remarriage, acceptance may not come easy for either you or your newcomer, especially if there are cultural or other major differences. But we need to try and to trust that as we get to know our new family members over time we will work our a healthy relationship or at least a modus vivendi.

The greatest danger comes from the dissatisfaction which leads to open and bitter objections or outright rejection. And this does happen. We are human, and sometimes we cannot restrain ourselves, even when we know it is counterproductive. More commonly, though, damage is done, not by rejection, but by disapproval, whether frankly spoken or simply hinted at. If we communicate this rejection—and we kid ourselves if we think we can really hide it—we push our children and those they love away from us and the family.

Though there are many different kinds of families, there is still one constant—each person's need for self-esteem. Self esteem comes not only from within, but also from our perceptions of how others, particularly our parents and our family, value us and accept us. These perceptions are so important that psychologists have given it a name: *validation.* All of us like to believe that the people who are important to us accept us, warts and all, in each stage of our lives. We are always balancing our need for autonomy—*I must define myself*—with our need for acceptance—*but I also need your affirmation.* Above all, your children need this acceptance from you, their parents, just as you needed (and perhaps still need or want) the acceptance of your parents.

Validation is especially important if children have broken off an old relationship. Even if the decision was a good one, life is not easy for them right now. They may be questioning their previous judgments, feeling a certain sense of failure, and even grieving for what they have lost. They need your help in coming to terms with themselves and their lives. We can ease their transition if we accept their choices. We must recognize that they are now in different stages of their lives, and that it will be easier for us as well as for them if we can help them get on with their lives. We can even be quite selfish in our motives, because the less stress we place on them, the less stress we impose on ourselves.

Commitment or Love?

Acceptance and validation are fine, but what about love? Love certainly is an essential ingredient in family life, but it is not the only ingredient. Popular psychologists (not to mention song writers) may too glibly say that "all you need is love" to keep a family together. Irving Kristol, publisher of *The National Interest,* disagrees. "Families," he says,

> are not about "love" but about sensed affection plus, above all, absolute commitment. Children do not yearn for "love," they desire and need the security that comes from such an absolute commitment, spiced with occasional demonstrations of affection. That is why children are so incredibly loyal to parents and grandparents who, by Hollywood standards, may seem to be unloving.

Whether or not we agree with Kristol's views, commitment is a necessity in this new world order of the family. Love is an emotion, something that even the most powerful of royal families have learned cannot be decreed into existence. But commitment is an act of choice, always within our power to make. There is a lesson here even for those of us who don't buy all of Kristol's thesis. We can't guarantee love for all the people our children bring into our family. But we can give them the absolute commitment and security that help our children make good choices in their own lives.

We may never be able to help them make correct choices. After all, who can say what the correct choices are for another person? Suppose we told our children what was correct...and life proved us wrong. They would still have to live with the possibly terrible consequences. And so, for that matter, would we.

What we need to give is intelligent support. That does not mean we have to regard everything that has happened as progress. Each of us will have our own opinion about that. If we are upset, it is understandable. In fact, just because we've been around longer and are more experienced in the ways of the world, we may be absolutely right in our judgments even when we are hoping that we are wrong. For the time being, that makes no difference. We have to acknowledge the situation that exists and accept it. The alternative to reject our child is not acceptable. We want to give our offspring what all of us crave, the knowledge that we are truly loved for who we are and what we are.

If we remain supportive and keep in mind the goal of fulfilling our commitments to our children, we can help them live the productive, happy lives that they choose to live. This does not mean that we must suspend our judgments about the paths they have chosen. But it does mean that we must acknowledge that these are their choices to make. We can only embrace our children, focussing our private attentions on what we think is good in their lives and overlooking what we don't like but cannot change.

CHAPTER II

Family Bonding

We are all sensitive to criticism. We don't enjoy it when someone points out our faults or reminds us of our past or present mistakes. We know only too well that we are not perfect...but who wants to hear it?

Children, even adult children, are particularly sensitive to our criticism, especially if they feel they haven't lived up to our expectations. After all, the emotional bond between parent and child is perhaps the most intensely sensitive bond in our lives. We are always and inextricably bound to each other. To our dying days, most of us will want parental love and approval. It goes with the parent-child territory.

Bonds Do Not A Prison Make...Or Do They?

While our emotional bonds remain strong, our family ties have become weaker. As we have seen, the structure of the family is changing. If there has been a divorce, children can have two sets of parents, half-brothers and sisters, and step-brothers and sisters. Sustaining family ties is more difficult when we live far apart. The need for two incomes to achieve a good standard of living means that children spend less time with their parents. The parent-child relationship exists, not in a vacuum, but in a real world that is becoming more and more diverse. Our children have gone to school with, lived with, and now work with people who are quite different from themselves. All along the way, they've been educated to accept this diversity.

Mix increasing diversity with looser family ties, and what is the result? We have less influence and control over our children's lives, including whom they date and wed. It's not surprising that the people they live with and/or marry can be quite different from our expectations.

And, let's face it—we do have expectations for our children, including expectations about whom they bring into the family even on a temporary basis. We want them to pair up with someone who is not only worthy of them, but someone who will also reflect well on us. We are not entirely selfless where our kids are concerned! It is satisfying to oh-so-casually drop into a conversation something about our daughter-in-law, the attorney or the doctor, or our son-in-law, the professor or the successful executive. And if we are really cool, we don't hesitate to mention that our daughter is living with a well-known television producer or that our son is living with a successful artist.

Most of us would never be so gross as to mention our children's income, but we're not above mentioning that they've just bought a house in an expensive neighborhood, or that they only shop in the best stores, or that they vacation at the poshest of resorts. We may even disapprove of what we consider their extravagance, but that doesn't always keep us from making sure that people know they can afford these luxuries.

If you're pleased with the mates your children have chosen, consider yourself fortunate. If you're also pleased with the in-laws they've acquired, you're doubly blessed. If these in-laws also find you very compatible and happen to have a boat, a summer home, or a Manhattan apartment with a guest room—your cup runneth over!

But, what if you're not pleased? What if you believe your adult child is heading for, or is already in, a relationship or a marriage which is unsuitable to a degree ranging from 'probably not a good idea' to 'totally unacceptable.' It could be co-habiting (as the Census Bureau might say), living in a gay or lesbian relationship, or marrying someone from a different ethnic group, religion, or race. It could be a marriage with silver cords (children from a previous marriage) attached.

Join the ever-expanding club of parents all over the country who are faced with similar problems.

Consider the Allen family, whose daughter shares a loft with her unstable boy friend. When the Allens visit, they try not to see the cat playing with the dust balls on the floor or the pyramid of unwashed dishes in the kitchen. They did sort-of laugh at her story about the bathroom which got so dirty that a stray popcorn seed sprouted. Or the Barker family, life-long activists in civil-rights groups, who found themselves sitting stony-faced at family dinners while their son-in-law insulted all minority groups. Or the Charles family, whose son's answering machine constantly shielded him from the dinner invitations of eligible women until he ended up marrying a woman with a five-year-old daughter and an unwillingness to have any more children.

Negotiating The Family Minefield

Like these parents, you may be upset and/or angry. Beware. You've just entered a family minefield. Tread carefully if you don't want to regret it later.

No one will say that staying calm, open-minded, and objective at this point is easy. As we muddle through life, we acquire a certain framework, a mindset, that influences how we live our lives. We have our opinions, ideas, and standards that are dear to us, that we are comfortable with, that suit the way we live. So what if they are not the latest or the trendiest? They're ours and they're us. Then something happens and we're asked to overlook these principles and ideals. Why should we? *We are perfectly comfortable, thank you, the way we are.*

Worse, we may even be asked to discard some of our ideas, to reassess our standards. It is natural to react with resentment, anger, and hostility, not only to the new person but also to our own son or daughter. If there are stepchildren involved, our feelings—and we don't like to acknowledge this mean-spiritedness—may even spill over to them.

For most of us, change is upsetting. It's human to resist. But what if our mindset is based upon old ideas or obsolete concepts which no longer fit current reality. What then? Psychologists say that we have to 'unlearn' our old ideas in order to learn and adopt new ones. If we can't break with these unrealistic or outdated ideas, we'll have a great amount of difficulty adapting to new situations.

This is, in fact, one of the dilemmas many of us have encountered as we have learned to cope with the new problems of our broader society. We try to be open-minded and humane, and we believe we are. We sympathize with the homeless, we recognize the need for day-care for children, we feel compassion for the emotionally disturbed. But when some government agency or private group wants to build low-cost housing units, a day-care center, or a treatment facility near us, we often become NIMBYs. Yes, but *Not In My Back Yard*.

We can become family NIMBYs as well. We believe in free choice and religious tolerance. We think it is all right for a woman to decide to have a baby if she's not married and even to plan to raise it herself. It's fine when a younger person decides to marry someone from a different race or religion. But it's not the same thing when your son brings home his fiancée of a different color or your daughter announces she's decided to have a baby fathered by the sperm bank. Sirens sound! Bells and whistles go off! Please...NIMF! *Not in My Family*.

Then, we're asked to be reasonable, not emotional, and to sweep away some of our prejudices. And, objectively, most of do have prejudices. They are easy to come by and not always easy to be aware of. Name any group—African-Americans, Catholics, Fundamentalists, Italians, Jews, Whites, Latinos, Gays/Lesbians—and it is easy to find something we can choose to call objectionable. All the world but thee and me, after all.

Of course, it helps if the someone about whom we have doubts is attractive, pleasant to talk to, and apparently good for our children. It's easier if the relationship seems to be reasonably equitable. It's more palatable if the new person seems to make our child happier. Status is a plus that reflects well on the family. Money certainly doesn't hurt. It may not bring happiness, but money does bring comfort and security.

Still, it is not easy to overcome prejudice. Just look at the world around us. Our attitudes have been ingrained over a long period of time. We should not feel guilty or ashamed if we can't overcome them quickly. It takes as long as it takes. Furthermore, along with our own prejudices, we may have to deal with and overcome the disapproval and social pressure of relatives and friends. But prejudice can be conquered and we are wiser people when we refuse to give up the effort.

Time for a Reality Check

What can we do? No more than the best we can, and this begins when we accept the world the way it is, not the way it used to be or the way we wish it would be. The reality is that we are dealing with our adult children, and we cannot make choices for them. If we disagree, we have choices of our own to make. These may range from acceptance with reservation to complete rejection. Whatever we do, it will not necessarily be easy. These are, after all, emotional, anxiety-producing circumstances.

Paul Rosenblatt, a professor of family social science at the University of Minnesota, says that parents frequently react to what they consider a poor match with a critical, stressful, self-examination. Were we at fault? What did we do wrong? Was there something missing in our family? This second-guessing doesn't help to ease the strain.

Stop for a minute and review the past. It is true that we had the first shot at socializing our children, but from nursery school on, we've had lots of competition. Remember the women's movement, the civil rights movement, the peace marches? No-fault divorces and co-ed dormitories? Rock songs that celebrated drugs? Movies that should have been x-rated but weren't? Television shows that almost glorified violence? We are not and never have been the only influence in our children's lives.

Stop, too, and consider this. If you've raised a child who has married outside of your cultural, religious, ethnic, or racial group, you have done something right. You should be proud, says Professor Rosenblatt. You have raised a person able to respect people as individuals and accept someone with a different background. Your child is well-prepared to deal with the challenges of a changing world.

You may be absolutely correct in considering your son's or daughter's choice as unsuitable. Remember, though, that neither a bad relationship nor a bad marriage has to be permanent. It can end, and if it is truly bad, it probably will. This may take time and cause pain, but it can and does happen.

As Walter and Sally Grimes got to know their son's new girl friend, they found their initial reservations were quickly transformed into a strong dislike. It was difficult for them, but they resisted the temptation to say something to their son. It was painful, too, according to Sally, who said that her tongue was sore from biting it so often. Fortunately, their silence worked. In about a year, the affair was over.

There is yet another virtue in keeping your mouths shut. We had some friends who were forever quarreling, bullying, and belittling each other. We wondered why they ever got married in the first place, until one day the husband said that if their parents hadn't been so adamantly and loudly opposed to the match, they probably would have broken their engagement!

Keep The Door Open

Even if you and your children are seriously estranged at the moment, don't assume that your estrangement will go on forever. There are things to do and ways to act that can bring about change. The initiative may have to come from you, but you may discover to your surprise that your son or daughter also wants to be reconciled. The family bond works in both directions. If a rapprochement is to occur, what will make it possible is following one simple rule: no matter how serious the conflict, keep the door open.

This rule is simple, but it may not be easy to follow. Alas, our past is always with us. If we tried in the past to exert control over our children and met with resistance, our attempts today to control will likely meet the same resistance. If we have disapproved of our son's or daughter's previous decisions about career, friends, lifestyle, or whatever, we may extend our residual disapproval to the new partner (or so it may be perceived) with the same negative effects. In fact, we may be using our opposition to the partner to screen, even from ourselves, our continuing disapproval of our child.

Sometimes, according to Helen Coales, a therapist and social worker who directs the Atlanta Child Guidance Center, children too may have some unconscious motivations. They may actually be ambivalent about their choices, but these choices allow the children to put their parents in situations where they can be critical. The children can then take the 'other side' and rebel. Or, children with unresolved relationship problems with their parents may unconsciously choose partners who have traits the parents dislike. These decisions may represent attempts by the children to work out the continuing problems with their parents. Old patterns do exist. If there are unresolved conflicts, they will surface again and they will need to be dealt with.

Unhappily, for some parents, feelings become so intense that they do what Professor Rosenblatt warns against. They close the door. This was the choice of the Gordon family. Their son Philip, a successful young man in the computer field, fell in love with Maria. When she immigrated to this country from South America, she had little money and was unable to speak English. She worked all kinds of jobs while putting herself through school at night. Gradually, she advanced up the career ladder until she obtained a government position with responsibity for a million-dollar budget.

When Philip said they were engaged, his parents tried to dissuade him. They said she was marrying him just to get citizenship. It made no difference when Philip told them she had been naturalized five years before they met. When the couple posted their marriage banns, his parents went to the parish priest and tried, unsuccessfully, to stop the marriage. Their small wedding had a sad undercurrent: their friends were there but his parents weren't. They had broken off all contact, and Philip says with sorrow that he didn't see them or his younger brothers and sisters for four years.

Could he explain his parents' action? They clung to their prejudices, he says, and nothing would change their minds. It was not a question of being rational, because prejudice itself is irrational. "How can you 'prove' the 'worth' of a partner?" he asks. "You can't, so there's no use trying."

Finally, through the intercession of an uncle, the two families were reconciled. They're all glad, of course, but Philip says that "there's a big hole" in his life and in the lives of his parents and his brothers and sisters. Like Professor Rosenblatt, Philip says, "don't close the door on your children. All of you will live to regret it."

Keep The Dialog Alive

Why do people like the Gordons take such extreme action? Extreme anxiety, according to Helen Coales. Parents don't know what to do. The constant turmoil and conflict drains them of psychic energy. They resort to drastic action.

There are better ways to relieve the stress and hold the family together. Keep in mind, says Professor Rosenblatt, that the relationship between family members is always negotiable…as long as the door is kept open. Even in seemingly impossible situations where angry people yell at each other and barely tolerate being in the same room, people will eventually resolve their differences if they continue to talk. After feelings have been vented, anger subsides. Each person begins to see a little justice in someone else's viewpoint, and a compromise can eventually be worked out.

The key is to emphasize, not right and wrong—there may be no right or wrong in the conflict with your child—but the differences in viewpoint which all of you can live with. You may continue to disagree with your son's or your daughter's judgment, but you need to be willing to respect his or her choice. Your child, in turn, can show respect for your judgment, try to understand your objections, and make the changes he or she is willing to make. Tolerance on both sides relieves the stress that is inevitable when families do not get along. If young children are involved, you can make their lives less difficult at an otherwise painful time. That alone makes the effort worthwhile.

One leavening influence, in fact, is that there are grand-children now or there may be in the future. You will certainly want a relationship with them, and your children will want their children to enjoy the special love that grandparents offer. Nor is it wrong to recognize that at some point you may need a relationship with your children and their part-ners.

If you can, says therapist Coales, step back from the situation and ask yourself about your underlying reasons for doing what you are doing. Are they really valid? Remember that this dilemma is particularly acute for your child, who is being pulled in opposite directions. Instead of asking your child to make what could be a wrenching change, are there changes you can make voluntarily? This can lay the ground-work for a future reconciliation.

We also need to recognize the true dimensions of the conflict. Sometimes, the disagreement is not only between parents and child, but also between the parents themselves. If this is the case, don't let it color your dealings with your children. If you and your spouse disagree on how to handle a problem, do not speak for each other. Instead, make it clear that you are speaking for yourself.

You don't have to say to your child, "You are wrong." You could say, instead, that "You are different from me/us. This engagement, your living arrangements, our relationship with you/your wife/your companion makes me/us uncomfort-able. Can we talk about it?"

The important thing is always to keep the dialog alive. Your words may not bring an issue to an immediate resolution, but you will be creating or maintaining an opening. You will be building a bridge that can be crossed later to reunite your family when you are all older, more mellow, or better able to understand each other's viewpoint. The alternative may be to burn the bridge down once and for all.

There is no magic formula for resolving these issues. Be wary, Professor Rosenblatt reminds us, of thinking that there are quick and easy answers—do this or do that and everything will be all right. If you look for magic wands, you will find disappointment. This is not a process that can be hurried, and it is difficult to know in advance what is the right way to proceed. Each family is different, and each family needs to work out its own solutions at its own pace.

There is outside help, if you want it. Sometimes it is as close as a relative or friend. They are not likely to solve the problem for us, but they can act as liaisons between the two sides. Likewise, ministers, priests, or rabbis who know your family well can help. If the problem seems truly intractable, you can turn to social workers or counselors who have training in marriage and family therapy. Ask your friends and relatives for recommendations. Or get referrals from any number of clearing house organizations, such as the National Council on Family Relations (3989 Central Ave. N.E., Ste. 500, Minneapolis, MN 55421; 612-781-9331), the American Association of Marriage and Family Therapists (1100 17th St. NW, 10th Floor, Washington, D.C.; 800-374-2638 or 202-452-0109), or any of the local state, county, and city association of family therapists which are listed in your classified directory.

There are no guarantees. So many emotions, memories, conflicting values, and so much pain may be circulating on all sides that no one can predict what a successful outcome will be. But, we can say with assurance that success is only possible if everyone—parents and children alike—are willing to make the effort.

CHAPTER III

Bonds Without Biology

"Move away. You can't be in the picture," he told ten-year-old Johnny. "We want the men in the family together, and you're not in the family." Johnny was 'only' the stepson of one of the men. It was a psychiatrist in the family who excluded him!

"I don't have to clean my room, and I don't have to listen to you," said sixteen-year-old Nikki. "You're not my mother." Her stepmother dropped the subject, afraid to insist out of fear that she would be thought of as the cruel stepmother.

"Can one of you please find her a boyfriend?" said a long-time member of the stepparent support group. "Then she'd stop calling my husband every day to remind him he's still Bobby's father, even though Bobby's living with her."

The Contemporary Stepfamily

This is just a small sample of the many problems that people in stepfamilies have to face daily.

Those of us who have never been in stepfamilies—and our numbers are shrinking—don't always understand how different and complicated step-lives can be. We're more apt to be influenced by the pattern of past decades, when stepfamilies were usually formed as a result of death. Stepparents were expected to take the place of the parent who'd died, and most accepted the responsibility.

Not so today, when fifty percent of marriages or more end in divorce. Stepparents don't replace the biological parents as much as they take a place alongside them. According to Professor Paul Glick, formerly of Arizona State University, if all of the people living in steprelationships are counted (stepparents, stepchildren, stepsiblings, stepchildren not living with parents, stepchildren aged nineteen or older, etc.), almost one-third of the U.S. population is or has been in a step family. If current trends continue, this one-third is expected to rise to about one-half by the year 2000.

Divorce doesn't mean giving up the quest for the pot of happiness at the end of the marriage rainbow, nor does it mean the end of parenting. Most of the once-married, with or without offspring, try it again, giving us new words in the language of love. Remarriage and co-parenting may not be found in many dictionaries yet, but they define familiar facts in the lives of many of our children.

Trying again is not always easy. There is often the feeling of personal failure—*how could I have been so blind/stupid/foolish/reckless/short-sighted?* Everyone has his or her own favorite self-accusatory word for the errors of the past. It is also difficult to get back into the dating game when you are older, fatter, less adventurous, and out of practice. Nevertheless, about eighty percent of the newly single go after the "triumph of hope over experience" and remarry.

Our try-again children remarry with the happy scent of new beginnings in the air. And why not? To start with doubts is to start with a self-fulfilling prophecy. We know from experience that marriage requires both personal adjustments to trivial disagreements, like how the dishwasher should be stacked, to major compromises about more serious things, like spending money or raising children. Our children know this when they contemplate or enter into remarriage, but they're likely to believe that they've learned from experience and that this time it will be different.

Time will tell whether this optimism is appropriate or not. For divorced singles, finding a wife or a husband is the realization of a dream. For single parents, having another adult to share the parenting is a blessing emotionally, physically, and financially. Parents and friends often think *Hooray! They're back to square one, a married couple again!* This may be wishful thinking. Instead of: 'square one,' the remarried couple is at the bottom of a pyramid facing a long climb. They will need time and help to make it to the top as a newly bonded family.

Stepfamilies And Stepchildren

Children can complicate this process considerably. What our newly re-wed children need to appreciate—as do we—is this: having children from previous marriages results in a complex web of relationships which make second marriages very different from first ones. Different and difficult. Just ask a family who is living through it.

According to Dr. Judith S. Wallerstein, the founder and former executive director of California's Center for the Family in Transition, modern stepfamilies are much more complex and undefined than the family of yesteryear. The role of the stepparent is vastly different, particularly because the biological mother or father of the child remains a force in the child's life. The presence of children makes building a second marriage much more challenging than building a first. And, she notes, children make sound second marriages all the more crucial. "The stakes are higher. The risks are greater. And everybody knows it."

The children themselves are not the cause of the tensions and stresses in the remarriage, strains that lead to about a fifty-percent divorce rate among second marriages. Rather, as soon as you add another person to any situation, you add complications. "Two's a company, three's a crowd." In a remarriage, the 'crowd' may include his and her children, who may be living together some or all of the time as well as ex-spouses who are still parts of their children's lives.

Add to these the legal ramifications. Biological parents and stepparents have different legal responsibilities. And financial questions. Who pays what, when, and how much?

On top of these, throw in the emotional adjustments. Think of the day-to-day adjustments you had to make as your children grew up, how you and they had to work at adapting to different personalities, talents, habits, even foibles. It is by no means easier with stepchildren. As hard as parents try to treat children equally, there is still an inevitable possibility of favoritism, misunderstanding, and jealousy. Family life is still family life.

These feelings can be magnified in stepfamilies, because parents, stepparents, biological children, and stepchildren (who may not have had a choice in the matter) don't have the luxury of time to learn to adapt to each other. Parents and children are thrust together to act as a family without having shared a family history. Family relations specialist D.M. Mills says that a biological mother or father has had five years to learn how to parent a five-year-old. A stepparent is always five years behind the natural parent in understanding and dealing with the child. And the five-year-old has to relate to a parent he or she hasn't grown up with.

The Real World Of Stepfamilies

Stepfamilies are different from first families.

Stepfamilies exist because of a loss and the pain that followed. Breaking a relationship means tearing apart old ties. Even when adults have chosen to sever these ties, it is natural to grieve. They have lost a spouse; they are single again; the dreams of the stable family they once thought they had have been shattered. Adults and children alike mourn the changes they have to make—the loss of their friends, the physical relocation to a new job or new school, the different lifestyle.

It may help us to understand stepfamilies if we recognize some of the myths about stepfamilies.

Myth: Love occurs instantly between the child and the stepparent.

Reality: It doesn't. Like any close relationship, it takes time to develop. Sometimes this can mean that your son or daughter is willing but the stepchild isn't. That hurts. Your son or daughter, and you too, may be angry and resentful.

Myth: Stepmothers are wicked.

Reality: Children learn about the evil stepmother in *Snow White* and the cruel stepmother and sisters in *Cinderella*. It may truly frighten them. The fear of being thought of as wicked may prevent a stepmother from acting in a child's best interest—enforcing discipline, for instance—for fear of antagonizing her husband by driving a wedge between a natural father and his child.

(While we're on the subject, why doesn't anyone ever criticize the fathers of Cinderella or Snow White? Where were they when bad things happened to their children? Are they the literary forerunners of today's delinquent dads?)

Myth: Adjustment to stepfamily life occurs quickly.

Reality: Stepfamilies are different kinds of extended families, with relationships that range from peaceful to bitter among stepparents, biological parents, and children. Experts say it takes from four to seven years for stepfamilies to work out their problems and establish good relationships.

Myth: Children adjust to divorce and remarriage more easily if biological fathers or mothers withdraw.

Reality: Children know that they have two biological parents. They adjust better when they are able to visit the nonresidential parent easily and when parent and child maintain a positive, constructive relationship. This can be a painful relationship for the nonresidential parent, but it is important for the emotional health and adjustment of the children.

Myth: Stepfamilies coming together after the death of one parent are formed more easily.

Reality: Both the widow and the widower need time to grieve and to accept a new spouse. The surviving spouse may find it difficult to be realistic about the person who died, sometimes forgetting his or her all-too-obvious faults. The new spouse may then find himself or herself competing with a ghost, an obviously unfair situation that can lead to conflicts in a new marriage or prevent children from accepting a new stepparent.

Myth: Part-time stepfamilies are easier to maintain

Reality: When stepchildren visit only occasionally, there isn't enough time to work on relationships. Part-time stepfamilies may take longer to achieve stability because stepfamilies need to go through various stages of development.

Stepparenting is also affected by the sex of the stepparent, the ages of the children, and the parent who has custody.

Kay Pasley, Associate Professor of human development and Family Studies at the University of North Carolina at Greensboro, tells us that women are usually the primary family caregivers. As a result, a woman who becomes a stepmother typically takes on more responsibilities for stepchildren than the typical stepfather in a comparable situation. Even when the children only visit their father while continuing to live with their biological mother, the stepmother is likely to have more responsibilities, simply because women more often than men run households and look after children.

A stepmother is particularly at risk, especially if she has no children of her own. She may try too hard too soon. She can be hurt deeply if the child, caught up in loyalty issues and simple childish fickleness, alternates between acceptance and rejection.

This is not so much of a problem if the children do not live with their stepmother while they are growing up. In *Second Chances*, Dr. Wallerstein reports that the children she studied had fewer loyalty conflicts simply because their stepmothers were not "serious rivals for the mother's love and devotion." Some adolescent girls can be drawn to a young stepmother and even become friends. If the stepmother has a baby, older stepchildren are often pleased to help care for the infant as long as they're not exploited as babysitters. Nevertheless, natural mothers almost always come out ahead of stopmothers in the eyes of children.

It is different with stepfathers. Some children may find it frightening to meet a man not related to them, one who hasn't shared their lives yet expects to be accepted as a parent. To the child, according to Dr. Wallerstein, "a stepfather is like a main character in a play who arrives in the middle of the second act." For the stepfather, there are no guarantees. "He may be welcomed as a rescuer, rejected as an alien, loved as a potential provider and source of love and affection, resented as an object of envy or hated as a potential rival."

The child's age when a parent remarries strongly influences the stepparent-stepchild relationship. In general, younger children, who are more responsive to adult overtures, are more likely than older ones to get along with their stepfathers.

The sex of the child also makes a difference. After the initial adjustments are made, girls are more likely to welcome their stepfathers into the family and to accept them as friends and parents.

Natural, nonresident parents may find adjustment difficult, as well. Absent parents—because children predominantly live with their mothers, these are usually fathers—often feel guilty because they are not able to share their children's daily lives, even though they may see them on weekends, holidays, summer vacations, and other times.

Real-life Stepparents

How does stepparenting work in real life? With difficulty.

Consider Susan, who wasn't particularly interested in getting married or having children until she fell in love with her husband-to-be, a divorced father of two boys, aged five and seven. When they were married, Susan understood that the two children would stay with their mother but live with their father and her during the summer.

In the beginning, she said, she "didn't know what to say to them or what to do with them." She couldn't draw on her own childhood with a "cold and distant mother." She didn't want the boys to call her "mother," because she knew she couldn't fulfill that role. Instead, she wanted them to think of her as an adult friend. She sent them letters telling about herself and expected that they would accept her. They didn't.

She bought books about dealing with stepchildren and tried to put what she read into practice. But in four years the relationship hasn't changed. There is a wall between them, she says, and she hasn't been able to break through. "It's like looking in a tool box to build something. What tool will fit? I haven't found the right tool yet."

Or consider Charles, a stepfather who has tried very hard to make friends with Hal, his ten-year-old stepson. When he moved in, he encouraged the boy to call him "Charles" instead of "Dad," helped him build a house for his pet rabbit, and chauffeured him to his scout meetings. Still, when Charles comes home tired after work and heads for the family room, Hal says, "Don't sit in that chair—that's my Dad's chair." Charles confesses to his stepparenting support group that he feels defeated.

Stepchildren, too, have their problems. They sense that stepfamilies are still perceived as inferior in some way to natural families. And they are not totally wrong. The July 1992 issue of *American Demographics*, for example, illustrated an otherwise sympathetic article on the problems of stepparenting with a picture of a farmyard with a family of three white and one black sheep. Or, the new edition of the *American Heritage Dictionary*, widely considered a definitive volume, defines a stepchild as *1. A spouse's child by a previous marriage. 2. Something that does not receive appropriate care, respect, or attention.*

Some children, ashamed they are in a stepfamily, try to hide it. When one little boy was asked in school to draw pictures of his family, he always drew pictures of his former family, not his current one. Another child's mother made her children stop calling their father "Dad" when he remarried. In another family, the: 'new' grandparents kept asking the children how they felt about having to go back and forth between two homes. The grandparents commiserated that "you must miss your friends," and "this must really upset you." The children got the message that something was wrong with their lives.

Unfortunately, there aren't any consciousness-raising groups for the world in which stepparents must live. Some stepparents have looked for a substitute for the prefix *step* as a way of changing their image in the eyes of the world. Perhaps a neutral word, such as *restructured* or *reformulated*, would help. (We frequently hear the word *blended* used to describe these families. But most stepparents know that they never really blend.)

This doesn't mean that they can't succeed—or that adults and children would be better off remaining in a bad marriage and unhappy home. As one stepfather told me, the key to success is the recognition that the stepfamily has its own rules and presumptions. Once this is accepted, stepfamilies can—and, even more importantly, do—fulfill that best-of-all-family roles of providing a place where children can be nurtured and adults can achieve a good life.

Where do we fit in this complicated situation? How should we react if our children are either considering or already in a remarriage?

We can help them by being supportive, or we can hurt them by being destructive. "We can build bridges or we can build walls," says Dr. Emily Visher, a stepparent who co-founded the Stepfamily Association of America with her husband John. Sometimes, through ignorance, not malice, we make the destructive choice.

As parents and grandparents, we can help our remarrying children and enrich our own lives at the same time. The next chapter discusses some of the supportive and constructive things we can do.

CHAPTER IV

Prefab Families And Instant Grandparents

So…your divorced son or daughter has just told you, "I'm getting married again." A big red question mark flashes in your brain: *What about the children, his, hers, or both?* You're about to ask.

Don't.

If you have your doubts—and many of us do—you could volunteer your opinion.

Just kidding.

They're Getting Remarried…Should You Celebrate?

Say, "Congratulations!" Obviously the decision has been made and your son or daughter wants your approval and support. If you can say it sincerely, the best comment to add is that you admire the new couple for accepting the challenge of a new family.

Later on, at a propitious moment, you can mention that a marriage always requires some high-tech-human-relationship juggling even when only two people are involved. With more than two, especially youngsters from previous marriages? State-of-the-art juggling.

But assume—and this is a mighty big assumption—that there is a propitious moment, and your child asks your opinion or says "I am thinking of getting married again." Can you actually offer some advice (the tactful word would be some suggestions)? Should you?

Only you can make that decision, based on your present relationship with your son or daughter. How open is it? Do you talk easily and frankly? Do you tread warily on a path filled with minor potholes from previous misunderstandings? Or do you cross a field of mines which can explode if one of you says or does the wrong thing? It is not an easy decision to make.

Even if you feel comfortable making suggestions, what could you say? After all, friends, relatives, even parents who have little experience with stepfamilies often don't know what to say or do. Typically, they aren't very helpful, at best. At worst, if they're critical or disapproving, they can be harmful.

You could, however, start with the obvious and encourage your children to find out what lies ahead. Suggest (diplomatically) that they read up on remarriage and stepparenting. Local librarians can refer you and them to a large shelf of appropriate books. Bookstores will have titles on the shelves or in the catalog.

There is a chance that your child may be rushing into this marriage. According to Kay Pasley of the University of North Carolina at Greensboro, what typically happens is that our son or daughter is lonely and/or unhappy. Then, your child meets 'someone special' and fall in love. There is a quick courtship. Why come home to loneliness or single parenthood when you can be with someone you love? They move in together, sure that they'll ride off into the rosy sunset. They don't always believe that a wagon train of problems might be following right behind.

They would be better off, says Professor Pasley, to prolong their courtship for at least a year (two would be better), to continue living apart, and to give children time to adjust. The more time before the remarriage, the fewer the problems of adjustment. Important child-related issues, like sharing finances and enforcing discipline, need to be discussed and settled in advance, not left to chance, according to Professor Pasley.

Understandably, an adult who is romantically entwined will not be overjoyed to hear this. Even suggesting a delay may seem to imply a form of discouragement. A more positive suggestion might be to recommend a support group for stepparents, particularly because a support group may continue to be valuable even after your child remarries.

A self-help group offers an opportunity to share experiences and problems with others who understand, because they've been there. One newcomer told a self-help group that he "felt like a jerk" until he heard what others had to say. Then he had what psychologists call an *aha!* experience— a realization that he wasn't alone, that others had similar problems which they hadn't solved yet, and that it was OK to ask for help.

Social psychologist Carol Tavris says that people in self-help groups are much better off, emotionally and physically, than those who try to face their problems alone. The sense of being alone, without support, can be devastating. What is more, according to clinical psychologist Marion Jacobs, self-help groups allow members not only to understand what is happening, but also to reinterpret it in ultimately beneficial ways.

The Stepfamily Association of America (SAA) is an important support-group resource, especially if stepchildren will be involved. It has about seventy local chapters whose meetings are open to all stepparents. These may be 'moan and groan' meetings, but they offer a valuable preview of the coming distractions. Susan, the stepmother from the previous chapter who hasn't yet chipped away the wall between her stepsons and herself, strongly recommended the SAA to anyone thinking of becoming a stepparent. Other stepparents quite agree on the value of SAA meetings. (Some have even said that they are not sure they would have gone ahead with their remarriages if they had attended SAA meetings first.)

SAA will send an information packet that includes a catalog of books and tapes about stepparenting and divorce, a one-page list of *Steps to Success,* and a brochure about the SAA. The Stepfamily Association of America, Inc. is located at 215 Centennial Mall, Suite 212, Lincoln, NE 68508 (800-735-0329).

After They've Tied The Knot

Fast forward. Your daughter or son has remarried. There are stepchildren of varying ages. And the wagon train has caught up with the couple who rode off into the sunset. What now?

The single most important thing you can do is to listen without being judgmental. Stepparents don't expect you to solve their problems. They know they must work them out on their own, even if they are your kids. Still, a brief respite and a chance to scream quietly without penalty is a wonderful relief.

While you are listening without judging, remember that a stepfamily is not a traditional family once-removed. It is a totally different kind of family. We parents and grandparents cannot deny these differences without compounding the insecurities and anxieties of the adults and the children in the stepfamily.

Just as there are myths about stepparenting, there are also myths about marriage. One of the most damaging is the 'happily ever after' myth. In their first marriages, we laughed when we noticed that our son stopped raving about his wife's gorgeous long hair after he had to clean out the trap in the bathroom. We chuckled when our daughter stopped admiring her husband's casual approach to life after she found his smelly socks thrown under the bed. We know that our children go through difficult times in their marriages. We can see the tight lips and the furious looks. We know that our wonderful grandchildren get into fights with their siblings, keep their bedrooms in shambles, slam doors after arguments, and sometimes hang out with unsavory friends. We accepted these as parts of our children's lives. We need to remember this when we see the problems in their reconstructed families. If nothing else, it will help us accept the hard times as normal.

The new family cannot be held to traditional standards. We can only view it in terms of the standards that the family sets for itself. For example, does it achieve its goal of having stable family relationships in the context of a strong marriage? There is no such thing as a standard mold from which remarriages are poured. The form the specific marriage takes will depend on the adults in the marriage and the personal responsibilities they bring with them.

All remarriages share common goals, however. One of these is to ease as much as possible the often difficult adjustments children have to make. Some typical examples include: the young girl accustomed to running around in her 'skivvies' who suddenly has two adolescent brothers; the six-foot teenager, who'd been the man in his single mother's household but is now displaced by a stepfather; the shy ten-year-old who must now spend weekends with two very noisy stepsisters. Who can blame these children when they make comments like *I like my Mom's house better* or *It was good before she came along* or *I don't want them to come here.*

If we can resist the urge to blame, we'll be more tolerant of what we might perceive as injustices or lack of gratitude and better able to understand the difficulties these children are having. Not that this is easy. If your son pays the college tuition of an adolescent who is unpleasant or downright nasty to him, you're naturally going to be annoyed. If your daughter denies herself the things she wants because her new husband has to contribute to the support of his children who are living with their mother, you're going to feel resentful. We are parents forever, and our children's hurts still hurt us, even if we disapproved of the choices that produced the hurts.

Unfortunately, the role of grandparents in stepparent families has not been researched very well. Even though the Stepfamily Association of America says that grandparents "assume new roles and can play an instrumental part in stepfamily success," many of us have no choice but to play it by ear and hope that we've been sensitively tuned in.

The process of becoming a stepgrandparent can be difficult. It usually goes something like this: when a son or daughter says they are going to remarry and children are involved, we typically react with shock and anxiety. We remember, with guilt, all the times we failed to give our children the attention and affection they needed while they were growing up. How can this son or daughter now take on someone else's children? Will our grandchildren have to share their parent's love with stepsiblings? Will we have grandchildren to carry on the family name? And, unspoken, who will inherit our estates? Sometimes, the long-buried *I-told-you-not-tos* and *you-should-haves* are resurrected, along with bitter arguments about which spouse was at fault for the son's or daughter's divorce.

We finally get to meet the children, who are dressed in their best and trying to not look scared. There are handshakes or hugs, too much fussing or not enough. And awkwardness. Grandparents and grandchildren need to work at establishing a relationship with one another for as long as it takes.

Names can be part of the awkwardness. Or, non-names might be more accurate. No one has yet come up with an easy, one-size-fits-all name for stepmother or stepfather, let along stepgrandmother or stepgrandfather. With good reason. While the names themselves are not important, they do symbolize the ambiguity involved in trying to build a relationship that has the ties and intimacies of a family without the biological basis.

Milly, a divorcée and businesswoman who raised her daughter as a single mother in the days when single mothers were rare, tells about the courtship and marriage of her daughter to a divorced father with two pre-teen daughters. Throughout the courtship, Milly happily reached out to the girls, but even as the wedding approached, the girls "didn't have a name for me that they were comfortable with." It was only just before the ceremony that "the girls took me aside and asked if I would be their 'official' grandmother. Could they call me 'Gran?' Immediately after the ceremony they came over to chat and must have called me 'Gran' 200 times that evening." What had distracted the girls hadn't been finding a name for Milly. It was being sure that the relationship was permanent enough to warrant finding a name. At last, they felt secure enough to choose a name for their 'official grandmother.'

The Challenge Of Being 'Real'

Names are symbolic. Being 'real,' on the other hand, is much more substantial in the world of stepparents. Stepgrandparents may not be certifiable in the eyes of some. In Milly's case, the other, well-to-do grandparents excluded her from the lavish family gatherings they hosted, because she wasn't a 'real' grandparent. When her wonderful son-in-law learned about the exclusion, he insisted on being the host so that Milly would be included.

'Realness' can be difficult for everyone in the family. Sometimes, it is the children who make the distinctions. When Cindy, a single mother, gets together with her former husband and his new family, Cindy's eleven-year-old daughter Peggy introduces the daughters of their father's new wife as her stepsisters and her fourteen-year-old brother as her real brother. Remember Charles from the previous chapter? His stepson Hal objected whenever Charles tried to sit in his 'real' Dad's chair in the family room.

Issues of authenticity can produce onerous distinctions. One stepfather's complaints illustrate how discrimination can result. "The grandmother of my wife's children doesn't treat my children as real members of the family," he says bitterly. Does she come out and say so openly? Of course not. But at Christmas she gives expensive sweaters to her grandchildren and packages of cheap underwear to her stepgrandchildren. Such unequal treatment of stepgrandchildren by grandparents is not uncommon. Sad to say, it is also hurtful to both children and their parents.

It does take time for emotional bonds to be forged. It is idealistic to think that everyone will easily assume the role of grandmother or grandfather. It is equally unreasonable to expect children immediately to accept their new stepsisters and stepbrothers. What parent who has had more than one child doesn't remember jealousy and sibling rivalry? These feelings can be intensified in stepfamilies. Grandparents should certainly understand this and accept is as quite normal.

In order to be accepted as real, grandparents need to act real. Send positive messages to children and grandchildren alike, affirming that they are as much a part of our families as we want to be parts of theirs. Where possible, we need also to avoid making the common mistakes that stepgrandparents often unwittingly make. Among the things we can do are:

- ✧ Introduce all children as members of the family, not as 'his' kids or 'her' kids. As Rita, a mother of three and stepmother of two, says, "If you would like to clarify the details of our family composition later, feel free to do so, but please introduce us as family."
- ✧ Send letters, cards, and gifts to the grandchildren when they are staying at their stepparent's houses. This sends the message that you accept these children as members of your family, regardless of where they happen to be living at the particular time.
- ✧ Understand that stepparents must act as parents, both nurturing and, when they need to, asserting authority and enforcing discipline. These are not the mythological wicked stepparents which were discussed in the last chapter. If we think they are making mistakes, we can discuss it with them privately (and this is good advice even in traditional families.)
- ✧ Put away our sympathy for the past disruptions to the lives of these children in stepparent families. Sympathy doesn't serve any useful purpose. These children need to accept the past as a fact of life, period. Instead, we

can strengthen their present by remembering their birthdays, going to their school affairs, taking them on outings, to movies, and to concerts. Well, maybe not rock concerts.

Maybe we could also set up a *Cupid Needs You* dating service for derelict ex-spouses, the ones who don't make child support payments on time, attempt to alienate children from the other parent, fail to keep appointments to pick up their children, etc. Let's make it so successful that all ex-spouses would remarry and become stepparents themselves. When it becomes their turn to face stepparenting complications, they will be much more understanding and cooperative.

The Bottom Line

What we really need to do when dealing with our stepgrandchildren (not to mention our own stepchildren) is to abide by the Golden Rule: *do unto others as you would have them do unto you.* Treat our stepkin and stepgrandchildren as we would want our grandchildren to be treated by their stepgrandparents.

Many stepparents say with sadness that "We know you will always care more for your biological family." For many, there's some truth to that, because we've had much more time in which to bond with each other. Most stepparents are not asking us to feel the same toward both. If we do, so much the better, but they recognize that we have known our biological grandchildren much longer and that blood ties cannot be ignored.

What they are asking, however, is that we be fair. We need to be inclusive, to remember that the children are innocent bystanders in the matrimonial skirmishes of their parents. This is important, not just for our grandchildren, but for our own daughters and sons as well. If we show favoritism, we not only hurt our grandchildren, but we ask our own children to choose among conflicting loyalties.

There will always be the pessimists who say the glass is half empty, not half full, and think that to be "perfectly honest"—and who needs this kind of honesty—they have to pour water out of the glass. There will always be those who say it is hypocritical to pretend to treat grandchildren equally.

"So what?" says Emily Visher, co-founder of the SAA, a mother of four and a stepmother of four more. "We're 'hypocritical' in our relations to other people all the time in order to smooth relationships when little is at stake." Where children's feelings about themselves and their places in the family and perhaps even the cohesiveness of the family itself is at risk, the stakes are so much higher. A little hypocrisy can be much kinder than a lot of brutal honesty.

When dealing in the subtleties of family (not to mention human) relationships, interpersonal reactions will be as individual as the people involved. Some of us will have difficulties in the beginning. Some, even with time, will always be uncomfortable. It may take a while, but some of us will love having additional grandchildren.

We need to remind ourselves that love is not a pie than can be divided unequally and serve only so many people. If anything, love is like a garden fountain, nurturing and watering its surroundings. We have the opportunity to form a different bond, one that is no less strong or delightful. Indeed, one that has its own special feelings precisely because it is by choice, not by biology.

If we are willing, we can be many things to a stepchild—a confidant, an adviser, an older 'grandfriend.' This is one of the most important things we can add to their lives, especially those of us who have been married for many years. When my husband and I celebrated our fortieth wedding anniversary, our stepgrandchildren were awestruck. We were an example of a special kind of loving longevity. We were proof that marriage works. We gave them hope.

We can be unabashedly selfish about this, too. Grandchildren bring diversity into our lives. As we get older, our friends get older, too. We know the punch lines of their jokes, their allergies, their politics. We love them, neuroses and all. But they don't add diversity to our lives. Grandchildren do.

Original grandchildren and then additional ones can be a welcome extended family. Through my six I've learned what it takes to put on a play; some of the fine points of football; how a *tae kwon do* expert can lie on a bed of nails and not get stuck; the hidden reasons why suburbanites donate to environmental causes; how to live on a minimum budget in Barcelona or New York City; and, as they say in commercials, much, much more.

For those of us who open ourselves and make the effort, the rewards are so much greater than the time and effort we expend.

What do we wish for our children? That, with or without our support, they will become successful "families of choice," in the words of Dave and Jo Driscoll. They have chosen to marry someone with a family, not by being fearful, but by being hopeful of providing stability for their children and each other. Happily, many are doing exactly that.

Our part is to show, by words and deeds, that we understand that new relationships can grow from newly entwined histories, that new loves can flower. And who is to judge the intricacies of these new relationships? The only thing that really matters is that they are being built.

CHAPTER V

Living (Dis)Arrangements

Our kids...They can be wonderful.

✧ *Bobby had just moved in after his divorce when I caught pneumonia. He shopped, cooked, cleaned, ran up and down the steps all day taking care of me until Jack came home from work.*

✧ *I was a widow with an eight-year-old son when I remarried. My husband and I were still feeling our way when his son dropped out of college and moved in with us. He became a big brother to my son.*

...But life isn't fair to them.

✧ *She sent a hundred résumés to law firms but didn't get any offers. Now she's working for a small law firm but not getting paid.*

...But life is too much for them.

✧ *We have a friendship with our daughters as well as a parent-child relationship. Still, we'd prefer it if instead of moving in and out, they would find themselves and decide what they want to do with their lives. Right now they have their feet firmly planted—in midair.*

...But they can be oblivious to the rest of the family.

✧ *He played his stereo at top volume all day!*

✧ *She knew I was orderly, but her room was always a total mess.*

✧ *They always ate dinner after we did…and left their dirty dishes in the sink.*

…But they have problems with their finances.

✧ *It was easy for him to be spoiled, living the way we do. He needed a car, but it didn't have to be a new one, and he got entangled in a couple of major credit-card debts. He makes in the mid-teens, but with the payments he has I figure he needs twenty or twenty-two thousand to be on his own.*

The Kids Are Back!

Welcome to the world of the RYAs and the ILYAs—the Returned Young Adults and the Incompletely Launched Young Adults, as they're affectionately named by the sociologists who study them. And study them they do—often first-hand in their own households.

In the popular press, the young adults who come home are called *Boomerang Kids,* since they so aptly fit the dictionary definition of a boomerang. As we shall see, their lives may be curved or bent, just as the wooden boomerang is curved or bent.

Do you have a RYA or an ILYA in your home at the moment? If you do, you're not alone. Almost half of middle-age (and middle-class) parents have one for a time, particularly when their kids are in their early twenties. To many parents, this togetherness comes totally unexpectedly.

Typically, when we were the ages of these children, we had jobs, career paths, often our own apartments, sometimes even our own progeny. Why are our children so different? So undecided about their lives? So late to get started? Surely, by the age of twenty-five, they should be on their own. But, according to the Census Bureau, in 1990 some twenty percent of women aged twenty-five and older, and thirty-two percent of men in the same age group, were not living on their own.

More men? That seems surprising. We think of men as more independent than women. And yet… Why should this be? No one has come up with a thoroughly convincing explanation yet, but there are a variety of candidates. Perhaps men expect to be cared for (and often are, especially by Mom) when they return home. Parents—fathers in particular—may be more relaxed when sons bring girl friends home for 'companionship' than when daughters bring boy friends home. Perhaps daughters are better at living alone. Or knowing that they will be expected to help out with housework may make them more reluctant to return home. Finally, if there is a divorce involving children, most of the time the mother will keep the home for the children and the father will move out, often to his parent's home.

The Not-So-Cheery World Of Our Children

The world in which young people are living doesn't make things any easier. Salaries have declined while housing costs have gone up. The job market has shrunk and many of the jobs which remain require more training than ever before. It's no wonder that young adults who have been living in roach-infested, plaster-peeling, cramped apartments look longingly at their cozy, comfortable, rent-free room at home. Add to this the lure of good home cooking instead of pizza and Chinese takeouts, a family car with an ever-full tank of gas, the sweaters ready for borrowing in Mom's drawer. Postponing marriage and coming back to the old homestead after college or after a life-crisis does seem like an intelligent move.

There is a ripple effect to all this. These decisions our young adults have made contribute to an uncertain job market and will continue to do so. Young singles don't need houses. If they live with their parents instead of buying or renting, they don't buy bedroom furniture, refrigerators, or life insurance. They don't pay utility bills or property taxes. If they don't marry, who needs real estate agents to show houses, bankers to arrange mortgages, or copywriters to write enticing ads? Plans for new houses never get beyond the blue-print stage, contractors close their offices, and entrepreneurs who might have opened restaurants and stores put their dreams on hold.

They stay single longer, too. In the 'good old days,' the advantages of getting married used to be (not necessarily in this order) sex, setting up one's own household, financial support for wives and domestic services for husbands. Nowadays, young people don't need the wedding band to get most of these advantages, and they can avoid one of the disadvantages, namely commitment. When and if they marry they are older. During the 1950s and 1960s, the median age of first marriage was twenty-two for men and twenty for women. By contrast, in 1992 the median age was more than twenty-six for men, while women averaged only a little younger.

Hoist By Their (And Our) Own Petard

This all adds up to what one demographer calls the 'new messiness' of becoming an adult in today's world. The emphasis is on the word becoming. People can be called adult only if they're independent. Our RYAs and ILYAs have not yet fully achieved that status.

Experts who study family relations and psychiatrists and psychotherapists who treat families with problems all agree that there are societal reasons for the RYA and ILYA phenomenon. We, their parents, can feel a little guilty, for we contributed much to the society in which these kids experience young adulthood.

We raised our children in families where life was centered on the child. This was the child-rearing philosophy of the educated, professional, managerial, middle class to which so many of us belonged or aspired. This was the family the books taught us was the ideal. Our children's feelings, wants, and needs were nurtured—some would say catered to—so we could help them develop to their full potential. We built what psychotherapists Phyliss Stegall and Jane Okimoto in their excellent 1987 book, *Boomerang Kids*, called a "childcentric world."

Our parents thought their life was full and successful if they raised their children and provided for their own retirement. In contrast, raising children was a very important part of our lives, but one with an unspoken yet very much understood time limit. We would have no 'empty nest crisis.' We had aspirations and plans for something else before retirement. The time limits and the 'something elses' varied from family to family. But we all knew that there would be a time for us after the children were grown.

This was particularly meaningful for wives. For married women, 'something else' began to take shape the day our youngest children started kindergarten or elementary school. It was time to get ready for the careers we never had or the careers we put on hold while we fulfilled our roles as mothers. We enrolled in record numbers in both undergraduate and graduate schools. We became a windfall to colleges with declining enrollments as we filled the seats left empty by the low birth rates during previous decades.

For many, there were economic incentives. We wanted our children to have college educations, yet we knew their tuition couldn't come out of our current incomes. We updated our résumés, brushed up on our business skills, headed back into the nine-to-five world, and started setting money aside for our children's college expenses. Sometimes, there were unexpected results. We discovered that we had hidden talents, that we were promotable, that being in the working world had not only financial but also personal rewards. We knew we would never go back to being 'just housewives.'

All this put added pressures on those housewives who were slower or less inclined to expand their worlds. They gradually found they couldn't get volunteers for their good causes, because so many of their contemporaries were now busy working their own jobs. They became tired of being the only women on the block who weren't heading in a new direction and earning money along the way. They found themselves chauffeuring the children whose mothers were working. And they began asking themselves: *Why should I volunteer? Instead of spending all these years fund-raising, organizing charity events, or planning luncheons, I could get a paying job.* Many of them went out and did just that.

Nor were husbands immune from examining their lives and their directions. If they were in business, they began to think about cultivating a future buyer so they could stop working such long hours. If they were doctors, or lawyers, or dentists, or accountants, they thought of taking a partner so they, too, might have more leisure and less pressure. Or, they calculated what their pensions would add up to if they left the corporation early to pursue totally different callings.

Our plans didn't exclude helping our adult children on a limited basis. We were happy to assist them from the sidelines, but we didn't plan to be the main event. According to Professor Allan Schnaiberg, a sociologist and a leading authority on families and the RYA and ILYA phenomenon, we parents took it for granted that we would have a life apart from our children, one that would be personally fulfilling.

The New Road to Adulthood

Marriage is viewed from a new perspective today. It used to be a happy way to establish independence from parents or (less happily) to camouflage the lack of independence behind the new dependence on a spouse. Now, young people, particularly young women, can get the same rewards by establishing themselves in careers.

Meanwhile, divorce has become a socially acceptable solution to marital problems. More and more young people have learned first-hand what it means to have their homes disrupted when their parents split. As they survey the trauma and debris of broken marriages, including the marriages of some of their friends, who can blame them for delaying the tying of their own marital knots? In the interim, many of them have stayed just where they were so comfortable—in the comfortable, familiar, and stable homes of their parents.

The forces which are changing the road to adulthood are not new phenomena. They have been around for some time. But now, what Professor Schnaiberg calls a "change in the opportunity structure" has reshaped the contours of our world and that of our children.

During the past sixteen years or so, young people have gone deeply into debt to pay their college tuitions—forty or fifty thousand dollars and up is not unusual for people going into the professions. Before they go out on their own, they've got to pay attention to their creditors. But how? At the same time, entry-level professional job opportunities have been shrinking, particularly in non-scientific and non-technical fields. And more jobs are requiring master's degrees and even doctorates to get a Reebok or a Gucci in the door.

Consider this the next time you dine out. You may well be enjoying the services of the best-educated dining-room staff in restaurant history, waiting on you while they wait for that professional job to open up.

Meanwhile, the expectations of the young have changed. Many of today's young adults now believe that good furniture, nice apartments, VCRs, microwave ovens, and stereo systems are necessities. (As we have seen, we may be responsible for encouraging some of these beliefs.) They simply don't know (or want to know) about orange-crate furniture, walkup apartments, or dinners made from leftovers.

We gladly gave our kids the things that many of us didn't have. We wanted them to have economic security, personal freedom, and comfortable homes. (Well, not totally. Sexual freedom was their idea. We never even dreamed about it.) But there was always an anticipated cut-off date. At the right moment our kids would happily fly out of the nest, get good jobs, and establish their own nests.

But what actually happened? Many of these 'fledgling adults,' as sociologists sometimes call them, tried their wings in the real world. Most of the prestigious jobs they thought were waiting for them proved to be figments of perhaps naive imaginations. For some, even the not-so-prestigious jobs were hard to find. Their marriages didn't work out according to their dreams. Living on entry-level salaries meant living a lifestyle they didn't like.

So they flew back into the nest. Some made it a way-station of sorts on the road to self discovery, flitting in and out as it suited their pleasure. Others flew home once, got their bearings, and left permanently. Still others never made it back out the door.

The Repopulated Nest

If this were a sociological treatise written for academics, we might be content with facts and figures. But statistics seldom tell about the impact on us, our families, and our children.

While some people find the transition easy, others find it difficult. In part, this is because we are all very different people. For all of us, different factors influence our abilities to adjust. In some cases, these arrangements have worked out well. Many parents are perfectly happy to have their unmarried children stay on the launching pad as long as they like.

Take Jeannette and Ira, for instance, whose daughter Lois got her B.A. in American Studies from a prestigious Eastern college but couldn't find a job in her field. She settled on a restaurant manager's job—temporarily—and moved home—temporarily—while deciding about graduate study. Jeannette and Ira "enjoy having Lois at home; it doesn't disrupt our routine." Of course, as Jeannette points out, they really don't see too much of their daughter, since she works nights and they work days.

Patricia's parents feel the same way. Their daughter was away for twelve years getting her M.D. Now she's ready to start her practice. Her parents think it would be "stupid" for her to pay rent while she's setting up her office. They have a big house, they work, and they have "many other interests." The only real problem was finding space in their basement to store her furniture until she could afford her own apartment.

For some, the old saw *Rich or poor it pays to have money* and its corollary *Rich or poor it pays to have a big house* ring true. Adjustment is much easier when there's lots of space, especially green space. It was no problem for one wealthy West Coast family, for example, when their son wanted to move back in. They felt he was too dependent and needed his own place if he were ever going to learn to manage on his own.

Their solution was simple. They bought him a charming small house not far from their own stunning, large house on the hilltop.

Would we could all afford this way out!

Space, though, is only one aspect of the solution, and often a small aspect. Human dimensions are much more important, as we'll discover in the next chapter.

CHAPTER VI

Real Worlds In Transition

Once, we expected that, when our children became adults, we could again think about ourselves as husband and wife. We looked forward to the time when we would be free from responsibility, the now–its–our–turn time to start careers or change them, to write checks to travel agents instead of college bursars, to eat in posh restaurants instead of pizza parlors.

The time after kids move out is a time when, according to family relations specialists Audra W. Clemens and Leland J. Axelson, couples can evaluate their relationships to each other and resolve issues which they chose to ignore or put off while the children were home. This is a time, many couples are delighted to discover, when they can experience again the freedom they enjoyed before the children were born and to rediscover the "more intimate, satisfying relationship which many studies indicate to be a by-product of the empty nest."

So, what happens when the kids return home? Some if not most of our expectations are suppressed, put on hold, or postponed. Not surprisingly, parents don't jump for joy when they cancel the trip, forget about converting a bedroom into an art studio, or examine the budget to see if they can afford a new round of tuition payments. Who can't understand the typical responses—resentment and anger, along with shame at having these feelings.

It is also normal to feel like a failure. Children believe they've failed because they're not independent, while their parents believe they've failed as parents because their children haven't done well. Accompanying these feelings is a loss of self-esteem among both the parents and the boomerangers. And, of course, there's guilt—as parents, we should have done better. (This guilt is not helpful. As we shall see, it can lead us to do things which are detrimental to our children.)

Yes…But

Despite these feelings, the real question remains. When your child asks, "Can I come home," can you really say no?

Most parents feel that they have no choice, that they have to answer *yes*. Very few parents say *yes…but*. Perhaps more parents should.

Consider Ed and Toni Smith, for example, who did say *yes…but*. Their daughter Suzie had been fiercely independent from her first ear-splitting cry in the delivery room. While Suzie was in high school, she had accumulated a solid bank account and learned how to manage money by working part-time as a teachers' aide in a home for developmentally retarded children. As a result of her job, she became interested in working with children, so after graduation she enrolled in an early childhood education program at the local community college.

Meanwhile, her ever-present determination to go her own way got even stronger. Suzie kept late hours and, her parents guessed, slept with a boy friend they didn't approve of. There were conflicts. Suzie wanted to resolve them by moving into her own apartment. "Go ahead," said the Smiths, "It's okay with us. But you're on your own; we're not going to pay for it."

For Suzie, this was not a problem. She switched from part-time to full-time, persuaded a girl friend to share the apartment, and quit college. Ed and Toni were convinced that she had made the wrong decisions about college, her boy friend, and her life style. But Suzie was self-supporting, so there was nothing more to do except—and this was an important exception—to maintain their family ties.

A year and a half passed. Suzie was now almost twenty, and her roommate had moved out. She couldn't manage the rent alone and asked if she could come home.

Yes…but. The Smiths replied. Ed and Toni spelled out the house rules, including one that Suzie could not come and go as she pleased without checking with her parents and another that she could not stay out all night. Toni remembers saying, "You would probably consider living here a fate worse than death."

"You're right, Mom." Suzie found a smaller apartment and soon afterwards a new boy friend who moved in. Luckily he was a solid citizen who persuaded Suzie not only to finish college and get her degree, but also to marry him. For all of them, it was a happy ending to a story that began with a simple *Yes…but.*

Do Parents Really Have Choices?

Most parents would probably feel, along with Robert Frost

> *Home is the place where, when*
> *You have to go there,*
> *They have to take you in.*

Especially when Frost adds:

> *I should have called it*
> *Something you somehow haven't to deserve.*

I put the question to sociologist Allan Schnaiberg. Is it true that since our children have no other place to go, we parents really have no choice?

Maybe so, said Professor Schnaiberg, but "it's not a package deal. There should be terms of the trade." He compared the situation, jokingly, to negotiations for a Volkswagen and for a Mercedes. What kind of costs do you obligate yourself to pay? Do you buy the package outright?

Do you want to pay a small price for a limited time with the Volkswagen or a higher price for a longer time with the Mercedes? You negotiate.

More seriously, he added, when parents say they have to, they're sometimes obscuring real problems. Just because the youngsters have been away from home—in college, or the armed forces, or apartments (often subsidized by parents)—doesn't mean they've really become independent. The truth is that many times problems don't show up until after the kids have returned home. We may not be doing our children any favors by automatically extending them run-of-the-house privileges, especially if we end up slowing their growth toward independence.

This doesn't mean that problems will necessarily show up. There are some kids who really must live at home or return home, but only so long as they need to. Many have well-defined goals, definite times when they expect to leave, and life plans they intend to follow. There are young adults like one of my grandsons, who chose to go to a law school close to home, after being away at college, so that he could save money by living at home. Forget these kids. They're okay.

Then there are those young adults who've established themselves only to find that they have become de-established by a weak or fickle economy. These are a new breed of Yuppies, those Young Upwardly Mobile Professionals who are now Young Unemployed Professionals. They may require some special handling, which we'll discuss in a later chapter. These young adults, too, are experiencing only temporary setbacks.

It is when our kids flounder that most of the problems occur. And unfortunately, it is the parents—you and I—who, in spite of our best past and present intentions, are responsible for many of the difficulties. As Albert the Alligator said in the *Pogo* comic strip, "We have met the enemy and he is us."

The Fault Lies Not in the Stars

What children need to grow up successfully is the stability that only parents can provide. And to provide it, parents must be in charge. What happens when they're not? When they let the children set the pace and have what Drs. Stegall and Okimoto call the "childcentric family"?

We all know families in which the youngsters never have to adapt to the 'real world.' When they encounter difficulties growing up, their parents always intervene for them. (How many mothers in the playground snatch Johnny or Jane away rather than let toddlers settle arguments themselves? How many fathers arrange for someone at work to type their kids' term papers?)

These Johnnys and Janes get to grow up thinking the world will be like that—when the going gets tough, they need only find somebody else to solve their problems and provide the answers. These youngsters are protected from disappointment, and this well-intentioned protection gives them a thoroughly unrealistic picture of life. They seldom get to experience the satisfaction or the growth that comes from overcoming obstacles by themselves.

It is often quite a shock to these youngsters when they find a real world in which other people not only refuse to let them set the pace but even make demands of them. They are truly unprepared. Sometimes, they can't face up to these pressures. Then, as all of us do now and then, they seek the comfort and reassurance of home, that familiar refuge and escape.

While children slip almost unconsciously into their old, dependent roles, parents, too, sometimes cling to their parental roles. According to Professor Schnaiberg, kids often get ambiguous messages. Many parents hold on tight while denying that they are holding on, and many of those who talk the loudest about wanting the children to leave are secretly clinging to the way things worked in the past.

These are parents who still want to control their childrens' lives, especially if they can't control some aspect of their own. They say *Go!*, then put obstacles in the way. "Why would you want to take a job like that? It's not right for you." Or, "You can't move there—it's not a safe neighborhood." Or,

"Of course we want you to get married, but that person isn't the right one."

Particularly if the parents' marriage isn't satisfying, children can be emotional crutches for their elders. According to family therapist Judith Algeo, a child at home can be a buffer; parents don't have to spend too much time with each other if they still have responsibilities to children living with them. These parents often can apply unspoken psychological pressures on their children. Professor Schnaiberg tells of students who came to him and said they had to go home. Their parents were about to be divorced, and the kids got the message that they were needed at home to bolster one or the other parent. One of my own journalism students informed me that she had to fly home immediately because her divorced mother had just told her that her father had moved in with a much younger woman. Though journalism, not psychology, was her major, she understood immediately that this was a blow to her mother and that she was 'needed' at home.

These are extreme cases. But they illustrate that parents can affect the child's decision to move back home. Unfortunately, they can also affect the child's natural progression toward separating from parents. This is especially true when the parents have very different viewpoints that have never been resolved.

Parents Also Have Conflicts

Consider the Watts family, Jim, Mary, and their daughter and three sons, all of whom went through college on Jim's salary. On the surface, they seem to have a story-book relationship. He recently retired and has a sizable pension on which they live comfortably in the suburbs of an East Coast city. Their home is well furnished. Jim tends the yard while Mary grows the flowers. He loves sports and she enjoys church and its social activities for women. They are both healthy. One of their neighbors calls them role models for the young families on the street—the ideal, happily retired couple.

Mary is surprised to hear this. Her life is quite different from what she expected and far from her ideal. Until about five years ago, it was pretty much what she had anticipated. Mary had taken it for granted that she would live a traditional life. She would marry, work for a while, quit when the first child was born, and then stay at home to be wife, mother, homemaker, and ultimately grandmother. After she married Jim, she did "make my opinions known but would know when to shut up. That's how women did it in my generation."

Jim grew up with similar expectations. He did exactly what he 'knew' he'd do: graduate from high school, get a job, get married, become a father, work hard, and get promoted. His wife would tend to him, their house, and their children, who would live at home until they got married and moved out. His daughter would follow in her mother's footsteps and his sons would follow in his (even down to his love of sports).

Mary assumed that their children would marry while in their twenties and then leave the house to build homes of their own. Their daughter and eldest son did just that. When their two younger sons also moved out, John to join the Navy and Peter to attend college, Mary began to enjoy her uncluttered home, her newfound privacy, and her simple routine of keeping house for only two.

But their lives began to diverge from her expectations. When John finished his Navy stint, he came home, settled happily in his old room, and got a fine job. He'd always been a "very good child but not one to socialize," and the Navy didn't change him. When his sister asked if he thought of going out on his own, he laughed and said, "I have no plans to move. It's like living at the Ritz with room service." Then Peter graduated from college with a degree in education. There were no jobs for teachers, so he took a decent job selling electronics. Peter had a big college loan to pay off, so he came home to save money. He, too, showed no interest in leaving.

Mary never expected that her sons would stay at home after they were adults. "I just assumed they would want to be on their own, like their sister and brother." She has "given up" on John but has "hopes" for Peter, who has a girl friend. In the meantime, "I'm doing for them just the way I did when they were young children."

It was difficult for Mary to return to her previous routine of waiting on her family. At first, when John and Peter moved back in, there was "war." She "yelled and screamed" at them to keep their rooms tidy and the house neat. "If they opened three letters on the dining-room table, there would be six pieces of paper lying around, the three letters and three envelopes." The boys would listen politely, but they didn't change. Jim didn't interfere. "So what good did my complaining do? All it did was make everyone unhappy. If I'm quiet, only one person is unhappy."

So Mary gave up.

Had there been any discussion before they came back about how the household would be run? Any rules laid out? Never. They were adults in a male-dominated house, and they assumed that they were entitled to do as they pleased. The boys tell her they "love being home." They also love sports, an interest that binds them to their father.

One of Mary's biggest gripes is having to iron up to twenty-three shirts a week. Why? Do the men insist on it? Not at all. They're satisfied with the way their wash-and-wear shirts look. But Mary isn't. Jim takes it for granted she will wait on the men. Their old patterns continue, to this day. Neither Mary nor the men are willing to change.,

Change Is Possible

Change may not be easy or comfortable, but it is possible, even when parents disagree. Sometimes outside assistance can help.

Helen Barker says she welcomed the day her children left the house. Steve, her husband, "loved having his children underfoot." So, when their daughter Florence said she had dropped out of college, hated her apartment, and wanted to come home, Helen said, "Omigod!" and Steve said, "Sure, darling, come home right away."

Florence's brief stay didn't thrill Helen, but she accepted it. Fortunately, the disruption was minimal. Helen's reluctance was understandable. She had always been the one who took care of the children. She cooked their meals, did their laundry, and cleaned up after them. This doing-parent-and-taken-care-of-child pattern resumed when Florence came home. Florence stayed while she returned to college to get her degree in nursing. As soon as she was self-supporting, she left.

It was different with their son Lee. At the age of 19, he decided that he wanted nothing more than to play an electric bass professionally. So he dropped out of college and moved into a big house with some other equally talented musicians. That proved to be a brief phase in his life, one which ended, Helen says, when he learned that "you have to buy oil to heat a house, and you have to shovel show when it falls on your sidewalk." Lee, too, returned to his parents' big house.

As Lee got older and capable of supporting himself, Helen waited for him to say, "I'm going to get my own apartment." He never did. "And why should he," she asks, "with two rooms on the second floor and the third floor to expand into?" He would leave on very successful tours with a rock group, but he always came home to the wonderful services Mom provided.

Finally, tired of maintaining their suburban home, Helen and Steve decided to buy a condominium. To finance the purchase, however, they needed to sell the house. They upset Lee when they suggested it was time for him to consider having his own place. Not only did he refuse to go out on his own, but Lee also swore that he wouldn't move out even if they sold the home.

Helen's and Steve's relationship became increasingly strained as they disagreed about how to deal with Lee. Finally, they sought help from a psychotherapist. They followed her advice: tell Lee that their plan to move didn't mean they didn't love him. They understood his distress and didn't want to upset him because they cared for him. But they needed a less stressful lifestyle, and that meant getting rid of the maintenance and expense of their house. The condominium had two bedrooms, so he would always have a "second home." But he needed a "larger first home," his own place. They would postpone their move, but only for a certain length of time.

Eventually a furious Lee agreed to the move. As of one day before moving day, he still hadn't found a place to live. Then a friend called and said he'd found an apartment for Lee, who took it sight unseen. His friends formed a last-minute "caravan across the desert," moving his belongings piece by piece. Helen says, "I didn't know whether to laugh or cry."

Now, seven years later, Lee says, "It was the best thing you ever did for me."

Moving In With Single Parents

Single parents may not have to settle different viewpoints with their spouses, but this doesn't save them from their own problems—and only one set of shoulders to bear the burden. Their own background influences how they deal with their boomeranging kids.

Consider Maggie. Early in her own stormy marriage but already the mother of a daughter and three sons, Maggie had gone to her well-to-do parents and asked if she could come home. "No," said her mother. "I love to have you visit, but you are not coming home. You are a married woman. You made your bed, now you have to figure out how to lie in it."

Maggie finally divorced her husband when her youngest son was twelve. The children attended good schools in a prestigious Connecticut town, so they stayed with their father in the family's fine home. Maggie moved to a one-room, studio apartment in a grand old Manhattan apartment building which was originally built for opera singers. The studio came with a balcony and had enough space for the usual furniture, including the computer work station Maggie used to support herself with free-lance editorial assignments.

One by one, as they got older, all four children, along with three cats, came to live with Maggie. If the weather was bad, it was mattresses on the floor. If the weather was good, the boys preferred to bed down in sleeping bags on the balcony, sixteen floors above one of Manhattan's busiest avenues.

The youngest son came when he was admitted to a New York high school for gifted children. The two older sons got jobs but continued to move in and out and out and in. "I thought of going down to a *Schrafft's* restaurant while they were remodeling," Maggie says, "and buying one of their revolving doors." Her daughter was the first to become self-supporting and move out permanently, though eventually all of them made the break.

Maggie never thought of saying, "No, you can't come home. It's crowded and I'm busy supporting myself." Why? "I felt I put my kids through a lot, and besides, they were quiet, agreeable, good kids."

At one point, after being on his own for about a year, the second son came home again. "There was something he needed from me," Maggie said, "and he was determined that he was going to get it. After a while, I realized that he'd gotten whatever it was he needed, and it was time for a change. I laid out the house rules, gave him a set of keys, and said 'from now on we're going to be independent roommates.'" Soon after, he left, the youngest son went off to college, and Maggie and the cats were happily on their own.

Even Trauma Can Help

Sometimes it takes a traumatic event to resolve family problems, as it did for Paul and Janet Ashton and their three daughters. Paul was a very successful reporter with a very influential newspaper. Janet had a successful real-estate consulting business which she ran from her office at home. The girls had all graduated from college and were living on their own.

Paul and Janet thought that it was finally time for them. They had worked hard, stashing money in the investments that were going to pay for their retirements in about ten years. They were enjoying their freedom from children. Despite their busy schedules, they made time to go to the theater often, dine out with friends, play tennis (Paul), and take up tap dancing (Janet).

But things changed. Their youngest daughter, Louise, found that her public relations career had much more pressure than she had anticipated. Her center-city neighborhood was deteriorating, crime was on the rise, her apartment was burgled, and her car was stolen. It was too much for Louise. She decided she hated public relations and that she wanted to teach school instead. That meant, however, that she'd need support for several years of room, board, and tuition.

Could Paul and Janet say no to a daughter who was unhappy in her career to the point of illness? Of course not. So, for the first time since she'd gone away to college six years earlier, Louise came back to the room in which she had grown up. The room was the same, but she was not. She took it for granted that she would schedule her own meals, set her own hours, and decide for herself when or even if to come home after dates.

Janet and Paul, however, hadn't changed their parental instincts. Janet reverted to being the same mother she'd been before, keeping microwavable dinners on hand for Louise for the times when she and Paul were eating out, dropping Louise's clothes off at the dry cleaner, and worrying about where her daughter was and why she wasn't home yet. Paul criticized Louise, who was quite attractive, for dressing in the current styles. He considered them so provocative that he worried she'd be raped on her weekends in Manhattan.

For the most part, their disagreements seemed like the predictable, minor differences of opinion between two generations. In reality, however, there was a lot that stayed just beneath the surface. Parents and daughter were like tectonic plates in an earthquake zone, shifting underneath while everything on top seemed stable. Until...

One week before Christmas, Janet and Louise had begun a mild disagreement which soon escalated into a shouting match. Suddenly, says Janet, "I realized I would lose control and say things I would be sorry for. I told Louise I didn't want to continue talking, went into my office, and locked the door. She followed me, banged on the door, and said she didn't want to stop. I refused to open the door. She began kicking it and, bingo, there was a big hole."

The hole broke the impasse between the generations. It scared them and made them stop to reevaluate where they stood. They discussed and, more importantly, accommodated. Janet and Paul realized they had to accept Louise as an adult who had the right to make her own decisions about her personal life, even if they didn't approve of those decisions. Louise realized she had to accept the constraints of being an adult in an adult home, including sharing chores and adapting to the family's schedule.

Janet and Paul asked Louise to pay for repairing the door, and she agreed. It was proof of her willingness to accept responsibility for herself. Janet was sure she'd never get a carpenter a week before Christmas, but a friend recommended a man who came around promptly.

When he saw the door, he grinned and said, "Your daughter did it."

"How did you know?"

"Experience. Sons punch a hole through the top. Daughters kick a hole through the bottom."

He added that when kids paid for the damage, he never had to return.

CHAPTER VII

Living (Re)Arrangements

The return of the adult child is not always smooth and uneventful. It doesn't have to be traumatic, however. There can be a lot of satisfaction in a successful return visit along with an admitted amount of discomfort.

First, the good news. Our returning children deserve credit for reevaluating their lives. They aren't continuing down a road leading nowhere. They realize they've made an incorrect career choice—it's hard to know what you want to do with the rest of your life when you're only a teenager—and that they need more time or more education to achieve their new goals. Or, they've had their fling with irresponsible living, want to grow up, and need help. Or, they've made a bad marriage, know it, and are building a better pattern out of the pieces of their lives.

There's more good news. Many families, after working out some initial problems of adjustment, find that living together again is not only tolerable but also downright pleasurable. The young folks don't require the care they needed when they were smaller. In fact, they provide help, companionship, and that special zing that comes just from having some youngsters around. They keep us up-to-date on what's in, who's a nerd, and what fashion is totally awesome.

You've had your sleepless nights, your worried days, and your guilty feelings. Now you deserve some credit as well. You did a lot of things right. You gave them the strength to make and carry out these plans. It worked before. There may be screaming sessions, angry looks, and bitter arguments when you lay down some rules and abide by them. But don't lose sight of what you deserve credit for...and why. Several years down the road, the same kids who are protesting your rules and limits will thank you and tell you that "you were right...again."

Now the bad news. You have to deal with the interim. It is small consolation to know that the experts—those psychotherapists and sociologist who claim to know all about these situations from all the research they have done—are not much better than you or I when it comes to handling these problems. Forewarned hasn't meant forearmed.

What Young Adults Need From Us

Guilt is a natural reaction. Even while you are anxious, angry, worried, resentful, or a combination of the all of them, you may also be feeling guilty. Don't! Put that feeling aside. It will hamper your judgment about the best course of action and keep you from doing what you should be doing.

Your successful negotiation of this passage begins when you first recognize what your young adults need from you at this point. The sad truth is that they are feeling some or all of the following: floundering, confused, embarrassed, injured, ashamed. One young man about to get a divorce and return home said to me, "It's bad enough to fail, but to fail in front of your parents is the worst."

What your kids need first is your empathy. Recall how you felt when you failed some major test in your life, or were rejected by someone you loved, or were fired from a job. This memory can help you get on the same emotional wavelength as your struggling son or daughter.

All our lives, we fight the battle between wanting to be supermen and superwomen, independent, strong, self-sufficient, and lovable, while simultaneously wanting to be nurtured, protected, and taken care of, preferably in high style. Young adulthood, the experts tell us, is the time when these opposing wishes are at their peaks. So, when your kids feel, deep in their guts, that they've failed, it's not surprising that they long to be children again and to have all the emotional and physical comforts of the home they remember from their childhood.

They may also fear failure again, wondering if they can ever make it. Your job is to offer haven and nurturing. And also to make it clear that you consider their situation temporary, a bump on the road to the independence they will certainly achieve. You will help them achieve it by standing with them as they develop or redevelop their competence. Alas, as much as you might yearn to, you cannot give them this competence yourself. You can only help them acquire it. Your role can only be to stand by, to bolster, to teach. But not to do it for them.

This is the challenge. It is so easy to slip back into the old parent/child relationship, the independent adult and the dependent child—that is precisely what you don't want to do. Resist that slippery slope. You will be doing a true favor for your children—and for yourself.

What should be your goal? To be out of work as a parent and to become an adult friend of your children. It isn't easy. (No one ever said that being a parent was easy, even after your kids are grown.) Don't start by asking the question *What should I provide for my children?* You'll be much better off to ask *What do these young adults need from me now?*

Keep in mind what the answer is not. Your kids do not need you to do for them. They need to learn how to do for themselves, and you can help them do that. When they learn this, they will not only be competent once again to deal with life, but they will also find their self-confidence and self-esteem are restored.

Consider Lisa, for example, in her late twenties, college graduate, divorced, no money, no job, whose only commitment was learning modern dance. Her parents had been divorced since she was twelve. From then until college, she lived with her mother. Kathy, her father's second wife, had met Lisa only three or four times. But she agreed with Len, Lisa's father, that they should take her in.

They agreed on certain ground rules. Lisa would have some responsibility for the house, including keeping her own room clean, and make a minimum financial contribution—at one point five dollars per week. Len and Kathy, in turn, would respect her privacy. Arguments would be settled quietly without shouting or berating. "I made up my mind," says Kathy, "to be very frank, to talk turkey. I told her if I said I would do something I would, and I did. But when I got to know her I loved her, and that made a difference."

Len and Kathy waited for Lisa to go job hunting. When she didn't they shared their concern and persuaded her to get therapy. The therapist urged her to get a job, to go out "into the cold, cruel world." She could continue her dancing after work.

Lisa looked elegant and got a saleswoman's job at a very fashionable dress shop. Getting ready for her first day, says Kathy, was a "major event." Kathy stood by while Lisa, under her supervision, slipped into one of Kathy's black dresses instead of the usual jeans and shirt, put on lipstick, and combed her long black hair into a becoming style. "Do I have to do this every day?" she asked. "That's what it's all about," said Kathy.

On her way to work, Kathy would drop Lisa off near the shop. After several days of being late because Lisa overslept, Kathy left without her one morning. Lisa was furious, but later told Kathy that "as the day went on I realized you were right. I used to get away with things." There were other arguments but no changing of the rules.

After a time, Lisa was fired for being late (lateness, carelessness, and procrastination are common among return-ees). This was a sobering experience. So was having to pay for damages to Len and Kathy's car when, late for a job interview, she drove a little too recklessly. Sobering enough, in fact, that over a period of months she improved, found a better job, took her own apartment, and successfully started toward her present career as a psychologist.

Len's and Kathy's blend of empathy, patience, and firmness helped bring their back-to-the-nest experience to a successful conclusion. Other families may not work out the challenge quite so easily. But persistence does pay off. Consider the Radners, another blended family consisting of Dan, Dan's twenty-year-old son Steve, Dan's second wife Isabel, and Kevin, Isabel's eight-year-old son.

For four years until Steve went away to college, he and Dan had happily shared a 'bachelor's pad.' When Dan and Isabel married and moved in together, Dan ran his book business from the study in their apartment. They'd been married about two years when Steve dropped out of college and needed a place to live. There wasn't enough money to subsidize an apartment for him, so without hesitating Dan and Isabel invited him to live with them. The study became Steve's bedroom and Dan's office moved to the kitchen.

Had there been any prior discussion? No. Dan was afraid to alienate his son, and Isabel was afraid to alienate Dan. "We tiptoed around each other." One important saving grace was that the two boys hit it right off, and Steve became a big brother to Kevin.

For Steve and Dan, life was like their bachelor-pad days. Steve had the run of the house with no questions asked, in part because he was working and contributed something to household expenses. "He's not a taker," Dan says.

Things weren't quite so simple for Isabel. She spent many unhappy months without complaining, even when Steve and his friends took over the living room and Isabel "felt as if my home had been invaded." When Steve brought a girl home to stay overnight, Isabel was "shocked. I am still bourgeois, but fortunately it didn't happen that often." What really got to her, though, was being a captive audience to Steve's rock music at top volume. When it got unbearable, she would leave the apartment—until one day she summoned up the courage to buy him earphones.

finally, after about a year and a half. with a little push and some financial help, Steve moved out of the apartment and into independence.

Success Doesn't Just Happen

As Dan and Isabel look back they are astonished, and pleased, that their marriage is still strong. But they believe months and months of difficult living could have been avoided if only they had thought and planned in advance about the living arrangements.

Take a cue from the parents who've had the easiest adjustments, those who realized ahead of time that they'd evolved lifestyles which a returning young adult, no matter how adorable and how loved, would have to disturb. You the parents need to discuss in advance how you're going to handle the situation. You need to find a solution ahead of time which allows for the welfare of everyone.

Your discussions should address any and all potential sources of difficulty. Certainly, the following questions should be answered:

How will the household be run? What kind of help should you expect and require?

Are you going to help financially? If so, for what and how much? Tuition? Paying off debts? A wardrobe for job hunting? Car payments?

Will there be rules about parties? Will the rules include what time the parties must end, how loud the music may be, what is served?

How about friends? When your kids were on their own, what you didn't know about their hours or their companions couldn't hurt you. Now, you're going to find out. Do you want to set curfew hours or insist on a separate phone for your child's incoming and outgoing phone calls?

Or sex? How will you feel when your young adult brings home a girl friend or a boy friend to spend the night? Or how will you react on Sunday morning when the bedroom door opens and someone of the opposite sex says, "Good Morning"?

Sooner or later, these and other issues are going to come up. It is better to discuss them before homecoming day, when the discussion can be relatively dispassionate, than to wait until after the opening bell in a knockdown, drag-out fight. An advance look is an opportunity to clear up misunderstandings between you. You may have very different ideas about what is acceptable. You need to settle your differences or your returning adult will get a confused message. This is particularly true when it comes to sex (theirs and yours). If you're a single parent yourself, you may only have to consult with your self. But if there's a spouse or lover in your life, he or she will need to be considered.

It is important that you establish your own authority. It is, after all, your house and your fortune, so you are entitled to draw the bottom lines. Sometimes, this can be difficult to do, especially in the beginning when your offspring is hurting. Your natural reaction might be to say how can I ask her to do this or how can I talk about it when she's already upset?

Still, you must make certain decisions, and you need to start by clarifying your own guidelines for making these decisions. Life sets limits with or without your help. Perhaps the reason your young adult has not been doing well is his or her own failure to recognize these limits. What are you going to do if your child also fails to acknowledge yours? Fortunately, few situations are completely intolerable when everyone realizes that they won't go on forever. For your sake and even more for your child's sake, everyone must understand that the move is both temporary and subject to conditions. And once you have made these decisions for yourself, you need to discuss them openly with your returning child.

The road may not be free of potholes. A big pothole is the who-are-you-to-talk-you're-not-doing-so-well-yourself hole. In the heat of an argument, maybe even when you first start to explain the ground rules, your child may throw your own failures back at you. What do you do?

What you don't do is let your life or the judgments you make about it get in your way. None of us is perfect. Your marriage may not be strawberries and cream or meat and potatoes. Your finances may make your accountant shudder. Your housekeeping might win a *Bad Housekeeping Seal of Disapproval.* You might rarely do today what you can put off till tomorrow. You might feel guilty that this whole mess is your fault to begin with because you didn't do the right thing the first time around. Perhaps you conclude that you are not the perfect role model and for that reason hesitate to set up rules for your adult child to follow.

Forget it. You don't have to have your own life together to make this renesting successful. Keep your goal as parent in mind: to help your child learn (or relearn) how to get along in the world as an independent adult. Besides, it is not your life that is up for review. So what if you are not perfect? Failing or refusing to set limits and rules simply because you feel unworthy isn't going to help you or your child.

The return home is a necessary learning phase in the growth of your child. Treat it that way. This is a rare second chance for you to do what you perhaps didn't do right the first time around or to fine-tune what you did do right. The larger world sets limits and you have a duty, not just a right, to set limits within the world of your family. This is also your child's second chance to get his or her life together. You must make it clear, however, that it is in the context of rules—your rules—that this will take place.

Chapter VIII discusses these rules and limits.

CHAPTER VIII

Rules And Guidelines

What issues cause the most conflict when young adults return home? Surprisingly, it is not just the life-and-death issues that cause the most conflict. In fact, sometimes it isn't the big issues at all that get our adrenalin pumping. The very fact that they are big scares us and makes us cautious. It's the little ones that often cause so many of the problems. Here are the results of a survey in the sociology journal, *Family Relations,* illustrated with examples from my own interviews.

Cleaning and maintenance...
> *They won't even stoop down to pick up a piece of paper—they don't even see it.*

Time of coming and going...
> *He said "So long, folks" on Friday night and didn't show up again until Sunday. We were frantic.*

Uses of household resources...
> *I had prepared these wonderful hors d'oeuvres for a dinner party, and when I got ready to take them out of the refrigerator, more than half were gone. She and her girl friend had "nibbled" on them.*

Mealtime...
> *We tried the dinner thing to get him to come home and eat at our regular time. But he was a man by then, and we couldn't tell him when to be home.*

Money and spending...
He's home to save money, so we don't ask for room and board. And then he spends a hundred dollars for a racquet ball racquet.

Entertaining of friends...
When he brought girls home, he entertained them royally with candlelight in the dining room...while I stayed in my bedroom.

Rent and other charges...
It never entered our minds!

What Do The Experts Say?

Therapists and parents who've weathered the storms without feeling weatherbeaten offer the following pieces of advice.

Time expectations Did you know that your daughter stayed at the local pub until 3:00 AM.? That your son slept in his girl friend's dorm room while you paid the bill for his dorm? Of course not, and it may be just as well. Your young adults consider the hours they keep strictly private business and any questions about them an invasion of their privacy. You can bet they will resent being asked *What time will you be home?*

You cannot set hours, but you can ask when they expect to be home, whether it's on the last train from the city or on Sunday morning after Saturday night's date. If you and your spouse have a routine for checking on each other's whereabouts, your kids might be willing to accept a similar routine. It is fair to say that you'd like to be able to contact them if they will be gone for some period of time. This is simply acknowledging that we live in a dangerous world, that smart people take precautions, and that parents still worry.

Cleaning and maintenance There is nothing wrong with insisting that shared rooms be kept orderly. Your idea of order may be different from theirs. You may even differ from your spouse. One person's mess, after all, is another person's lived-in look. Still, it is fair to set minimum standards and to insist on keeping them. This is no more than young adults are asked to do when they share common areas with others who are not their parents and no more than they will have to do on a job.

(Untidiness may seem to be a universal characteristic of today's young adults. Why? Take your choice: [1] They are less materialistic than we are...[2] We didn't stress neatness when they were growing up because we were afraid of spoiling their creativity...[3] It's their way of resisting authority...[4] They didn't work as hard as we did to get their worldly goods, so they don't appreciate their value... [5] We were neater because we never had that much to throw around...[6] They're just plain slobs, but that's not our fault and we love them anyway.

My granddaughter Miriam offers the following examples of the way her college friends treat people who don't do their part to keep shared areas clean. They collect the trash or garbage left by the culprit and put it on his/her bed; they put the culprit's name on the garbage and put it in his or her personal space; they confront them with the evidence [used condoms, for example], point out that it is their mess, a health hazard, disgusting, and insist that it never happen again.)

Chores You also have a right to expect the sharing of some chores. If it is the accepted rule in your family that assignments are just made, go ahead and make them. If that is not your style, you might find it easier to let people pick the jobs they want to do. Or you might have a lottery; make a dart board with jobs on it and let everyone throw a dart; rotate jobs so that everyone takes a turn with the unpleasant chores. The point is that everyone in the lifeboat has to pull an oar occasionally.

Eating and mealtimes Some families fit easily into previous patterns of dining together. Many do not. For those who don't, the best way seems to be to let family members fend for themselves. Give your children their own shelf in the refrigerator. They stock it with their own groceries if they're working. It is also quite reasonable to expect that those who fend for themselves will also be responsible for doing their own dishes. One family said that having their daughters eat out or cook for themselves actually "saved the day."

Sex We take it for granted that young adults have sex without, pardon the archaic phrase, 'benefit of clergy.' (It is so accepted that when friends of our granddaughter's planned to visit for the weekend, she warned us to make special arrangements—this young couple *didn't* sleep together!) These days, the question is usually not *if?* but *where?*. There are no easy answers. Should parents permit it, pretend not to know what is going on when they are away or asleep, or forbid it in their homes?

Some say *Not in my house!*—so daughters spend the weekend in their boy friends' apartments (and complain about the filth). One couple accepted having their son's sweetheart sleeping over occasionally in his room. But when she was going to spend a month with them, they insisted that she sleep in the guest room. Yet another family said, "How could we say no, when intellectually we accepted premarital sex." (And, besides, they really loved their daughter's boy friend.)

Money: The Root Of Many Problems

Most of us, as our own parents used to say, are "not made of money." We have our own presents and futures to worry about. Sure, we gripe to each other about money—maybe we even gripe to our closest friends about money, too—but not to our children. Ask our kids for room and board? You've got to be kidding! A contribution to cover the additional expenses? It rarely happens. This could be, says psychologist Marcia Halperin, just the same old parental wish to go on giving our children the advantages we never had.

There are sound psychological reasons for hesitating to talk about money (more of this in Chapter xxi, below). Money is power and reflects on the parents' self-esteem. Parents may resent having to give money to their children once again, and they feel so guilty about their resentment that they suppress it. Neither of these attitudes is in the best interest of the child, who can't be independent unless he or she can be self-supporting. There has to be a time when they learn about financial limits—and it's never too late for this lesson to be mastered.

How do you go about assessing whether your young adult can contribute to the family coffers? You start by avoiding confrontation, or at least whatever your child will perceive as confrontation. Don't just blurt out "What's with your finances?" They will certainly become defensive and just as certainly view this as an intrusion.

A better way, says Dr. Halperin, is to say that "finances is a problem (or a question) for us as a family." Then, within limits, explain your situation and ask how the young adult can make a contribution. Both the amount and the time frame should be discussed. For instance, if your child has no resources at the moment but anticipates getting a job in the future, you could set a cutoff date after which he or she is expected to chip in. How much will depend on earnings and the other financial commitments your child has incurred.

Another possibility is to ask the young adult to barter services in lieu of money. This has a psychological advantage. Your child is not a taker but a giver, and this can be important for his or her self-esteem and self-respect.

How about the kids who come home with debts, par-ticularly debts run up on credit cards? The immediate advice is the same as you'd give any credit card junkie. Keep one card, preferably the one with the lowest interest rate and/or the lowest annual fee. In our credit-based economy, one card is essential, since it is often required for identification or car rentals and to obviate the need to carry lots of cash. Then cut up the other cards and learn to live the pay-as-you-go life.

Judith Lau, a nationally known financial planner, offers valuable suggestions for thinking about money. Her advice to clients recognizes the psychological aspects of money management as well as the strictly financial components.

Lau acknowledges that parents want to help but that they also want to establish a positive keel for their young adults. What they don't want to do is perpetuate the problems the child already has had in dealing with finances, especially when these problems may be based on misguided feelings of entitlement. "You've got plenty of money," the young adult may say, "so why don't you just pay off my debts?"

Especially if you are reasonably well-to-do, this can cause a real guilt trip. Stand back, Lau advises, and look at what you are trying to accomplish. Certainly you want to give them a respite, but you also want to strengthen their foundation. It will be easier if you keep in mind that you're not always going to be around, or even able to bail them out if you are. If you haven't helped them learn to be responsible, you are the irresponsible one. (Don't start feeling guilty again.)

It is tempting to say, "We'll (or I'll) pay off your loan and you pay me back." Don't. Instead, help your young adult set up a budget (call it a financial plan if the word budget is threatening) that will allow some kind of payment schedule. If your child has no income, this could provide the push for getting a full-time or even a part-time job. At the very least, plan for an exchange of work around the house or garden in lieu of payment.

If you need further encouragement, consider again how the young deal with financial problems when they are living together. Do they allow free rides? Of course not. So why should you?

Outstanding debts do have to be settled. Ms. Lau recommends that you and your child talk to the creditors and restructure the payments to a level that your son or daughter can afford. These days, she says, creditors are very willing to work with debtors if they only will come in and talk.

Another possibility is to have the young adult consolidate all credit card debts and pay them off by getting a loan from a bank with a set time limit and affordable monthly payments. He or she should shop around for the best terms—this is an education in itself. One real benefit is that the interest rate on such a loan will most likely be lower than the interest rate on the credit card bills. You will almost certainly have to co-sign the loan and/or put up security, so by all means make sure your child can be trusted and is capable of making the payments.

(I teach at a college where bulletin boards are full of invitations for students to take out credit cards. This makes it too easy for students to become credit-card junkies. It doesn't absolve the student of responsibility for using the card wisely, but credit card issuers should also bear some responsibility for being the dealers who get individuals hooked.)

There are credit counseling offices around the country which are skilled in helping the real credit-card junkies. These are non-profit agencies which offer their services for free. Sending a young adult to one is a reasonable option. However, heed the word of caution from Thomas A. O'Neill, president of the Consumer Credit Counseling Service of Delaware Valley. Encourage your child to do this on his or her own, but don't do it for them and don't come with them to the office. If you do, your child may feel that the counselor is "telling this to Mom or Dad, not to me."

How does it work? The headquarters of these debt counseling services, the National Foundation for Consumer Credit, in Silver Spring, Maryland, has a national referral line (301-589-5600). Call this hotline to get the toll-free number of the nearest local or regional agency. This agency will then refer an individual to the nearest counseling service where your child can get an appointment with a counselor.

During the meeting, the counselor will help your child make a budget and set a realistic schedule for repaying debts. The young adult then makes a proposal to the creditors for repayment. Once the proposal has been accepted, your child will send an agreed-upon amount to the agency monthly. The agency, in turn, will manage the payment of creditors until the total debt has been paid. Some (not all) creditors may even reduce the interest payments or eliminate them entirely, which is an added benefit of going this route.

A significant advantage of this plan is that you are out of the picture. Your child is responsible. If you're smart and keep your distance, you can say goodbye to nagging and hello to peace-of-mind. Much more importantly, your child will have taken another step up the ladder of independence.

Doing Our Part

You may be out of the picture in these financial arrangements, but you're very much in the picture when you and your child share the same home. Living together is much more complicated than abiding by house rules, as we all have learned. No one expects complete bliss, but everyone wants and needs, if not a bit of heaven, than at least some earthly satisfaction.

When we ask our children to live up to adult standards of responsibility, we have to be sensitive to their feelings and adapt to them just as we would do with other adults. (Seriously. I shudder now when I think of some of the liberties I've taken with my children, liberties I wouldn't dream of taking with even my closest friends.) As perfect as we think we are, we may behave in ways that drive them up the wall without being aware of it. It's so easy to slip into the old routines. *Do you have your key?...Be careful driving!... You're not going to a party like that, are you?*

Our young adults have the right to ask us to make reasonable changes as well. If we stand on our 'rights' as parents and refuse, we may not be living up to our unspoken agreement to deal with them as adults. We have no right to violate the privacy of their rooms, for example, even if it means that the floor is paved wall-to-wall with dirty laundry.

Will the millennium arrive? We know better. Inevitably there will be angry feelings and conflicts. At some point, your young adult is going to be irritated, upset, curious, exasperated, disappointed, or frustrated. Accept this in advance and you won't be caught off-guard when these feelings are expressed through slammed doors, telephone receivers banged down, or sharp answers to harmless questions. It's your house and you are the nearest person, so you're going to be most affected.

Like all of us when we're going through difficult times, your young adult will be self-involved, less perceptive, or even totally oblivious to what other family members need, want, or are entitled to. You're human too. You're going to be angry and you're going to be tempted to attack, all of which brings forth familiar patterns of counterattack or withdrawal. Nothing will be accomplished.

The best way to handle anger is to say that you're angry and why, without threatening or attacking. Do it while you still have some control. Resist slamming the door yourself, and, if need be, just go away until you regain control. You don't want to say something you'll regret later.

Gilda Carle applies her Ph.D. in organization and administration to the anger-busting workshops she offers to major corporations. Her recommendations on handling anger constructively and getting positive results may work equally well outside the corporate structure. Here's how they would work in a family context.

- ✦ Tell your child the specific behavior that offends you (littering the family room, neglecting to write down phone messages, forgetting to put gas in the car.)
- ✦ Explain how this behavior affects you (everyone is forced to sit in a messy room; you missed an important message about the time of a meeting; you were late because you had to stop for gas.)
- ✦ State your feelings about these transgressions (the family is being imposed on; you've been embarrassed needlessly; you're very angry.)
- ✦ State the behavior you expect in the future (pick up the mess; write the message down and leave it where you will see it; put gas in the tank or tell you that you didn't.)
- ✦ After you've made your points, end the discussion.

This last step can be critical. Most people find it hard to walk away without dragging in other grievances. This can undo what you've just accomplished. "Learn to quit while you're ahead," Dr. Carle stresses.

The road to unpleasantness and recrimination is paved with good intentions...that are forgotten. Once you and your returning child have agreed on the rules of the road you're going to travel along together, follow the suggestion of one lawyer-parent: put it in writing.

A contract. It can be as simple as a written list. It can be done in exquisite calligraphy. It can be full of the whereases and wherefores so dear to the lawyer's heart. Regardless of its form, a written contract is one way to insure a successful renesting. Something about its impersonality actually adds to its strength. It isn't that your child didn't live up to promises to you, but that he or she didn't fulfill the terms of the contract.

The contract will be as varied as the people who draw it up, but it should cover all of the potential problem areas. Expand it to meet your own requirements. At the minimum, it should address questions of fair play (household responsibilities and mutual expectations), guests (who stays, when, how often, under what conditions), meals (when they're served, who does the shopping, who cleans up), and money (who contributes what and when, which services can be bartered for cash).

You are human and you are a parent. (As much as it may seem at times, they are not mutually exclusive.) You know that it takes time to change. You don't expect perfection immediately, or next week, or next month. But you do expect improvements, and you know that, with time, patience, and love, people do change. For the better. Be patient, be persistent, be supportive, and the time when your young adult returns to the nest can become a memory you will laugh about long after it has passed.

CHAPTER IX

TLC And Rx For The Unemployed

Life isn't fair. (What else is new?) We still call them Yuppies, those erstwhile 'Young, Upwardly Mobile Professionals.' But now, many are 'Young, Unemployed Professionals.' As we have seen, the loss of a job is one of the main reasons why kids return to the nest.

Life isn't fair to us, either.

The Newly Unemployed

Losing a job has its own special agonies. The displaced are among the unlucky ones who have been laid off, some twice in a year. Many had gone into debt to pay their college tuitions—or perhaps you went into debt for them. They pressed for success, studied hard, graduated, found jobs. If they were good, or fortunate, or both, they landed the jobs they wanted and trained for. If not, then jobs with possibilities, or at least jobs. They supported themselves while planning for something better in the future. And then... *Sorry, we don't need you anymore.*

Perhaps they knew the economy or their field was weak. Perhaps their entire group or department was laid off. It's still a blow. And it is humiliating to stand in the long lines to collect unemployment checks. As they wait, who can blame

them for thinking, *Why did I work so hard to get that degree?*
Why did I take out all those student loans? Now I'm stuck with
them, and I owe all that money. I could be in this line with just a
high-school diploma, no debts, and not be any worse off.

Most of these Yuppies have ongoing bills besides their
student loans. Many do not have very much in their savings
accounts. If they turn to their parents, they do so with mixed
feelings: they are grateful that their parents are there, but
they are embarrassed or ashamed at having to ask.

Come on Down???

If our kids have been living on their own, our first reaction
may well be to say, "Give up your apartment and come
home."

Is this the best thing to do?

"No," says Dr. Gilda Carle. Asking an unlucky child to
come home conveys the wrong message. When parents urge
a child to return home, they're often saying (or understood
to be saying) *I'm okay, but you're not...I manage on my own, but*
you can't. Or, just as disabling, *You don't have to manage on your*
own; I'll always be there to help you. Neither of these attitudes
reinforces the independence our kids need to have.

"It depends," says Dr. David Rice, clinical psychologist
and professor of psychiatry at the University of Wisconsin
Medical School. It has to be evaluated on the basis of your
past relationship. If a child has abused the relationship by
frequently calling on parents for help in difficult situations,
it is not a good idea. Echoing Carle's caveat, Rice points out
that parents who are always ready to step in are simply
perpetuating patterns of dependency.

At other times, though, Dr. Rice believes parents should
show their love and compassion by asking their children if
they would like to come home, even if it is unlikely they will
accept the offer. Kids may have financial or other valid
reasons for accepting the invitation. But, as we saw in the last
chapter, if the offer is accepted, parents need to make it clear
that the return home is not a return to dependency but an

opportunity to find some breathing space. Parents should set up or negotiate the terms of the return and encourage their child to get some kind of a job in order to remain as self-supporting as possible.

This advice is difficult for many parents to accept. We didn't raise our children to confront these kinds of difficulties. We forgot some of the lessons of the depression of the 1930s. During some of the recessions that have occurred in recent memory, professional and white-collar families were barely affected. During prosperous years, many of us were lulled into artificial security. But times have changed, both for our children and for us. We're just beginning to recognize that the value of our homes may have dropped permanently, that the interest income from our investments can drop, and that long-term jobs are not necessarily guaranteed.

The Best Response

How, then, should you respond when you hear about lost jobs? Ask your children what they need from you and if and how you can help. They will need both time and energy to figure out what to do. At the outset, while they're assessing the situation and making decisions, offer lots of care and concern. There will be time later for specifics and details—paying bills, making loans, finding contacts, helping with resumes, giving advice.

One of the most valuable things you can do is to listen without judging. Let your kids voice their anger, disappointment, and doubts about themselves, their future, and the world at large. Bite your tongue if the words *I told you so* even enter your subconscious. (*I told you not to major in ancient Yak rituals...I told you not to buy an expensive car...I told you to save your temp-job money instead of skiing the Alps.* None of these help.) To remind them of this past advice is to set up an instantly adversarial relationship, which is the last thing you want to do. Yes, you were right, but so what? That's no help now.

Remind them that they got jobs initially because they had talents and abilities. They were successful once, and they will be again. Even if they recognize that you are trying to give their self-esteem a subconscious boost, they will appreciate it.

You may not talk the same way to your son as you would to your daughter. Men are more likely than women to judge their self-worth by the size of their salary. If your son is going to be earning less than before, it may be useful to remind him that salary is not a realistic basis on which to judge people. His generation has developed a set of we're-not-materialistic standards, and he should abide by them. This doesn't mean that your daughter won't feel the same discomfort or even anger at having to settle for less, but she may not feel as strongly that it reflects her value as an individual.

You can avoid potential conflict by knowing what to expect. Your child, like anyone who has been laid off, may experience all or some of the following feelings at once or in succession:

Anger: "Why did this happen to me when I worked so hard?"

Guilt: "I should have seen this coming and started to look sooner."

Despondence: "I'm just not capable or talented or competent. I'll never get a good job again."

And finally *Acceptance:* "Okay. It happened. Let's get on with life."

These emotions may last for weeks at a time, and they may be difficult to overcome. They may need to be vented. Don't be surprised if your son or daughter takes to sleeping late, neglecting his or her appearance, taking offense at the slightest remarks, and in general being very hard to live with. And, of course, you are available for target practice.

You'll have your own anxieties and questions, as well. Is he looking for a job in a reasonable way? Are her expectations too high or his search too narrow? Are his salary demands unreasonable in the current market? Should she go for additional training? Switch careers entirely? What will happen when she can no longer meet her car payments. You may find your own reasons to be angry. Shouldn't he be working harder to get another job? Shouldn't she be cutting her expenses instead of continuing to spend as if she were still working? Why won't they listen when you give them good advice?

Before you confront your son's or daughter's problems, and especially before you offer your advice, you need to decide what is the most reasonable course of action for you to take. Is this the right time to suggest that your child go back to school for additional training? Or would a switch in careers be more appropriate and, if so, which career? How far are you willing or able to give financial support? Should you offer to take over your son's car payments, or should you urge him to sell the car? If you are going to offer money to help your daughter until she gets a new job, should it be a loan or a gift? And should you expect to have a say about the way it is spent, especially when you see it being spent in a way you disapprove of? Make sure that you and your spouse agree about what you are going to do. If the two of you argue, you will only add to the increased tension in your household and, even worse, make it easy for your child to feel guilty for causing the two of you to quarrel.

Don't be offended if your child seeks more advice from friends, especially friends who are also out of work, than from you or the family. There is no generation gap among contemporaries, so these friends are often able to make suggestions or even to be critical in a way that you can't. As one young adult reminded me, her unemployed friends were a great help when she lost her job. Besides bringing news of possible job openings they knew about, they had good suggestions on how to slant or improve her resume. Further, her friends had parents, relatives, and contacts who were additional sources of job leads.

Beginning The Transition

If you have relatives, friends, or colleagues who can offer some insight into the job market, particularly your child's job market, by all means call them. In the past, it may have been difficult to tell Uncle Joe or Edwina in the Personnel Department that Johnny or Janie is now unemployed. Perhaps you felt it would be an admission that you and your kids were losers, especially if *their* children (who had gotten into the job market a few years earlier) were successful. Well, these are the nineties. Now, everyone, including Edwina and Uncle Joe, knows that their kids could be next.

There are a few practical tips you can offer even before your child leaves the job. Recommend that your son or daughter make the exit in the most graceful way possible. This may not be easy. In times of anger or resentment, people may not feel like being gracious. But remind them, as my parents used to remind me, "leave a clean path behind you. You never know when you'll have to walk that way again."

Meanwhile, encourage your son or daughter to do the following:

- ⟡ Get information from the personnel department about severance pay, health insurance coverage, and outplacement services.
- ⟡ Ask bosses and supervisors for references and for letters of recommendation.
- ⟡ Leave a business card with them and offer to accept temporary assignments.
- ⟡ If possible, get names, titles, phone numbers, and any other pertinent information about the people they have had professional contact with—suppliers, consultants, other professionals, managers, etc. Leave business cards with them, too, in case they know where other jobs are open.
- ⟡ find out if the company is able to put a résumé in computerized data bases and other places where employers look for help.

Remind them not to bad-mouth the boss, the department, or the company. This can get back to former colleagues and do the cause no good whatsoever. Feelings of resentment or betrayal are natural, and unleashing a tirade of complaints can be very satisfying. Restraint is more difficult, but much wiser. The boss, the department, even the company may not have felt it had a choice, and the unfortunate decision may not have been personal. Buttoning one's lip may be difficult, but it is often the best strategy.

See if your child can be covered under your health insurance policy, even if only temporarily. If there are outstanding debts, encourage your child to write to the creditors, explaining the situation and offering to pay them (with interest, if necessary) as soon as he or she is working again. If he or she hasn't already done so, encourage your child to apply for unemployment benefits. Some people put off applying because of false optimism or shame, even though they are entitled to the benefits. This money can help them keep up with expenses, and it is a boost to their morale as well.

Is this going to be fun?

Don't order the party favors quite yet. But remember that your children will get stronger as they overcome this setback. They may not say so, but knowing you are there will give them great comfort, as it always has.

CHAPTER X

A Survey Of
Family Relationships

This is not an exam. You're not going to get a grade, although you've more than done your homework, and for that alone you deserve a gold star.

How would you answer these questions?

- ❖ *Describe your supportive/emotional relationship with your adult children. Is it reciprocal? Do each of you give something to the other, in a fairly equal way? Or would you call it unequal, i.e. one of you gives more than the other?*

- ❖ *Do you think your children sometimes take advantage of you? If so, how?*

- ❖ *Do you believe you were more respectful of your parents? If so, why?*

These questions were parts of a survey of parents from various parts of the country. This study included people from the East and West coasts, the heartland, and places in between; representatives of a variety of occupations and professions, including teachers, managers, administrators, retailers, lawyers, doctors, journalists, and others; men and women of all marital statuses (still married, divorced and remarried, single mothers and fathers); the employed and the retired; families just scraping by financially and others living well to living very comfortably.

The small but representative survey brought forth a whole range of answers. One still-married mother, a store manager, said, "I can't answer. Too many emotions, buried, would be dredged up if I filled out the questionnaire and then I wouldn't sleep all night. My daughter still reminds me she never got the Mary Jane shoes she wanted thirty years ago." Another respondent was a long-time divorced mother and a bank vice president who said, "My responses may not be what you are looking for and it may seem I have two perfect sons—but I answered from my heart. They are not perfect but they are very nice gentlemen, and I'm proud of them. And I believe they're also rather proud of their mother."

In between these poles were the other respondents—and the rest of us—who experienced relationships that were easy at times and difficult at other times, easy with one child and difficult with another. They felt put upon sometimes and willing to do more at other times. Most wondered—or knew with 20/20 hindsight—how they would do things differently if they had them to do over.

Many were surprised and pleased that past problems, after some heartaches, lots of worry, and growing maturity, seemed to have worked themselves out. Some were surprised and delighted that acquiring sons- or daughters-in-law sometimes brought better relationships with their sons or daughters. Others were surprised and disappointed that the acquisition brought unexpected and hurtful problems.

A few parents felt that all was well with their world, but, not surprisingly, many more felt some areas still needed improvement. Some had simply given up, while others had sought professional help from ministers, rabbis, psychologists, and psychotherapists. One father said, "I am not happy with my relationship with my son, but I am resigned to the fact that it is not likely to change." One mother said, "I do not think 'unfair' describes our relationship with our children— perhaps unfortunate [would be a better word]. I am trying to change [with professional help] by confronting some of our differences with them. It seems to be helping some."

The Timing Is Right

There are many reasons to ask these questions now. Because the gray hairs are coming in thicker...because the joints are beginning to creak...because the steps we used to run up easily are getting more and more steep...because there will never be a better time than now.

Because middle age brings mixed signals: eat cheese because it's got calcium for our bones; don't eat cheese because it's got too much cholesterol. Get out in the sun; at our age we need sunshine. Stay out of the sun; it causes wrinkles. Take an afternoon nap; it's good for you. Don't take an afternoon nap; it will disturb your nighttime sleep.

Because we've reached an important turning point of age. It's time to re-assess the business side of our lives—our careers, our finances, where we live. A time for planning the future and making some changes. A time to re-assess our relationships with others, particularly our children. Just as we want to do something about our out-of-kilter joints while we're still physically flexible, we want to make some changes in the out-of-kilter connections with our children while we're still independent and psychologically flexible.

Because we have passed a parent-child Rubicon. Though we still have obligations to our children, they're no longer our primary responsibilities. They're responsible for themselves now, while our primary responsibilities have shifted to ourselves and our spouses. We have changed our expectations about and for them. And they probably have changed their expectations about and for us, as well. If we are fortunate, these changes have followed parallel paths.

What makes this important is that we are now spending much more time as the parents of adult children. It's certainly much longer than the time our parents spent, simply because we're living longer and staying healthy and independent while we enjoy these additional years.

This doesn't mean that we'll act like the rational grown-ups we believe we are and get along just fine (except perhaps for a few minor tiffs here and there). That assumption is contrary to centuries of the history. Consider the Bible, Greek and Roman drama, the plays of Shakespeare, for example, if today's family seems too close to look at objectively.

Still, there have been changes. Attitudes, for example, were different when we were being raised. For our generation, there was no question that mother and father were Parents, with a capital P. They believed that their way was the right way, and we respected their judgments, in large measure because they were our Parents. As we raised our children, by contrast, we questioned ourselves. We wondered if we were doing the right thing in view of all the often contradictory expert advice with which we were bombarded.

We were not necessarily one, big, happy family in our parent's household. Our feelings were mixed, or so respondents to the survey remembered them. Among survey responses were statements like: "I was more respectful—I don't think any other way would have been tolerated"; "The times and mores were different but we were always fearful of hurting or bringing shame on them"; and "A lack of dialogue was considered 'respect'." A few offered the extreme viewpoint, "I thought they were stupid and didn't want to have anything to do with them." No one said, "We thought about them as 'pals.'" But they were our parents, and we respected them for that reason if for no other.

Respect is defined differently these days. It is not something that is necessarily owed, a duty to parents just because they are parents. Rather, it comes from an evaluation and appreciation of parents as individuals and as parents. This is a more demanding view, probably a more honest one, and in the long run, a more beneficial one as well.

One facet hasn't changed, however. Along with marriage, the parent-child bond remains the most important relationship in the parents' lives. Because this bond is so strong and because it will persist for the rest of our lives, it's very important, for our sake and that of our children, that this bond be as trouble-free as possible. If there are problems now, now is the time to pay attention.

By doing this, we accomplish many things. First and foremost, we make life easier for ourselves; there's nothing wrong with that. Simultaneously, we make life easier for them; there's nothing wrong with that either. Perhaps we can spare them the guilt that we may feel as we look back with sorrow now that our parents are gone. *If only I had said that, or done that; now it's too late.*

Easier Sought Than Found

Oscar Wilde once said, "When our children were young they loved us; when they got older, they judged us. When they are adults they may forgive us." Let's amend that to read, "When our children were young, we loved them; as they got older, we (and the world) judged them. Now that we and they are older, let us seek mutual respect understanding, tolerance, and if need be, mutual forgiveness."

This is what we aim for—but many of us haven't attained it yet. Here is what some participants in the survey said. A retired electronics engineer was sad that "My son tends to view questions or suggestions from me with a suspicious, 'what does he really mean by that?' attitude." A single mother lamented: "I wish they were more caring and sensitive. I worry all the time if they'll be caring, helpful husbands...or like their father." One mother said, "One day I asked both my daughters—on a scale of one to ten how did I rate as a mother? They both said they would have to think about it...Needless to say I never brought up the subject again." (Would you feel comfortable asking your children that question?)

A number of parents expressed regret and guilt about their past. "I got a divorce when my children were still in pre-school and moved them four thousand miles from their father. Then I gave them a stepfather they disliked intensely." "For career and financial reasons, because I was a movie and television reporter, I spent a lot of time away from home."

"I changed jobs and had to move to several cities. My son was forced to go to three different elementary schools in six years."

Others were worried that they had spoiled their children. Few parents felt they indulged their kids too much with life's big and little luxuries—no Mercedes-Benz to get to high school or cashmere sweaters by the dozen, for example. Many parents were proud that their children had paid at least some of their expenses by cleaning other people's houses, installing air conditioners, or waiting on tables.

But many were very aware that they had spoiled their children in other ways, making life easier for them in a manner that had consequences the parents hadn't foreseen and hadn't served their children well. As one college professor and educator said, "'Spoiled' is not the right word. We made a mistake in not giving our children enough structure. We needed to set boundaries. Now the kids are paying the price with problems they still have to work out." Another father said, "I think over the years we've spoiled our children by trying too hard to solve their problems instead of urging them to try hard to solve their own problems." And a psychotherapist and mother said, "We kept them from having to bear the consequences of their inappropriate behavior."

Many parents answered *Yes* to the question, "Do your children take advantage of your sometime?" Their familiar complaints ran the gamut: "Getting in touch usually means they need or want something...I sometimes feel like my son's secretary, doing things for him, without getting enough respect or help...I'm helping grown children financially and almost having the help taken for granted...They depended on us for considerable financial help and also expect a good deal of other help, but there's little flow the other way...They expect us to be there for them." One parent expressed what many respondents were feeling: "I'm afraid we brought up our kids to expect from us, but not to feel responsible for 'doing' for us. I would like to change and make it clear that consideration, responsibilities, and obligations flow both ways."

Finding The Two-Way Street

Most parents who said they had been taken advantage of wanted to see a change for the better. They didn't want to look back later and say, with disbelief, "We've done it again! There was a problem to be solved and we solved it by obscuring it or denying it." Instead, they sought ways to work it out that built a two-way relationship with their kids.

They also acknowledged that taking advantage didn't mean that feelings weren't reciprocated or that the situation was completely one-sided. They were bothered much more by the fact that the relationship was unequal, that they didn't know how to change it, and that they were afraid to risk losing their children's love by trying to initiate changes.

However, "'Unequal' is a bitter word," says college professor Jerry Allender. "Unequal is not the right word when talking about parents and children. A better word is 'balanced.'"

In the traditional view of the family, a certain amount of reciprocity between parents and adult children was simply presumed. If the need arose, whether from illness, the death of a spouse, or whatever, parents expected to find a place for themselves in their children's homes. If the parents had financial troubles, children were expected to lend or even give money. In case of illness, children (especially daughters and daughters-in-law) were expected to help with post-hospitalization care. Some families took it for granted that the adult children would not move far away so they could be called on for help and the families could continue to socialize.

Children did not always live up to these expectations. Nor were parents always happy to have to move in with their children. But almost everyone assumed that 'family' meant more than a little obligation.

Times have changed. Most of us shudder at the thought of moving in with our children, though we love the thought that we'd be welcome. Share a home, miles from friends and shopping, with rock music and a neurotic dog or haughty cat? Heaven forbid! Besides, most of our kids live too far from our part-time jobs, our volunteer work, or the college where we've enrolled.

Ask children to stay close when they can get better jobs in Miami, Los Angeles, or Minneapolis? Who would ever suggest it? It's a tough world out there, and we don't need to make it tougher. Besides, the same societal changes that have made it possible for them to accept jobs in Mexico City have helped us become seasoned travelers. We don't hesitate to hop in a plane for a visit.

Care during an illness or the recovery period? A lot of this has been taken over by trained professionals who can offer specialized services—such as home or outpatient physical therapy—that our children can't provide.

Financial help? Thanks to things like changes in real estate values, improvements in social security, Medicare, good pension plans, hard work, thriftiness, and sometimes just being in the right place at the right time, many of us are financially independent. We can cheerfully say, "Thank God, we don't need to ask them for help." In fact, as we'll see, we're much more likely to be givers or lenders, not vice versa.

We cherish our independence and expect it to continue for a very long time (is forever too much to ask?). We have different perspectives and different expectations about what our children should do for us. We can now have a more nearly equal, adult-to-adult relationship.

Or can we? We wonder if we haven't gone too far, if we haven't obscured or neglected the fact that equality among adults requires responsibility. The absence of responsibility produces inevitable problems, and it's to no one's advantage to let these problems fester and affect our relationships.

In the next chapter, we'll talk about how we weave our ever so intricate family ties, and why and how they sometimes get tangled.

CHAPTER XI

The Wobbly Parent-Child Seesaw

Who would have thought, the first time the baby delighted us by returning our smile, that this simple connection between us would get so intricate? Or when we were so proud that the baby learned to grasp a rattle, that the same baby would one day rattle us? In the beginning we understood our responsibilities; understanding their responsibilities comes only after a long apprenticeship.

"There is always a two-way flow of responsibility between parents and child," says Dale Jaffe, professor of sociology at the University of Wisconsin. But, precise amounts—so much of this, so much of that, how much we give, how much you give—can't be quantified on a neat little chart, as much as sociologists may try to. It's difficult, if not impossible, to generalize about relationships, says Dr. Jaffe, since "they are constantly being re-negotiated, depending on the situation at hand and the history of relations within the family."

What actually happens? In *Of Human Bonding*, the classic textbook of parent-child relationships from birth to death, sociologists Peter H. and Alice Rossi point out that the "grooves of parental habit [to help children] are in place," and not easily changed. In contrast, as children go through the various stages of their lives, they make tracks, not grooves, and they're not very deep tracks. Our kids are constant changing, and with each change they inevitably renegotiate their ties to and with their parents. Each new phase brings a different situation and a need for both parents and children to adapt.

Many of us haven't adapted as well as we could have. All of us should know from experience about the deep grooves of parental habits. Yet, how many of us continue to keep quiet when we ought to speak up, overlook slights that should not be overlooked, or rush to the rescue, though we shouldn't, when things go wrong?

The patterns of relationships within each family are unique. Nevertheless, a few general factors exert strong influences on how people in a family interact. According to Dr. Mark Fine, a clinical psychologist and chairman of the Department of Human Development and Family Studies at the University of Missouri, there are three important variables.

Gender of the child: In general, girls have closer relationships with their parents while growing up, and these continue into adulthood. They are taught to value relationships, to be more caring than men, and to be more family oriented. Men don't make, or don't take, the time for relationships in the way that women do. This may be less true now than formerly, but Alice and Peter Rossi say that women still do more "parenting than men, and anticipate both that they will be needed to help their families, and will, at some future time, need help from families."

Marital Status: Marriage brings major changes. Sons and daughters now have primary relationships to their spouses, not their parents, and parent–child ties can change substantially. If the sons- or daughters-in-law get along well with their parents-in-law, closer relationships can form; otherwise, the relationships can become more distant or strained. Some parents may feel that the bride or groom has taken away the son or daughter. One mother, telling of a somewhat strained relationship with her son after his marriage, said, "As most mothers feel, when their son gets married, some of the bonds between mother and son become 'unstuck'. This has hurt me very much."

Grandchildren: Their births tend to bring parents and children closer. Before grandchildren, the young marrieds may consciously or unconsciously distance themselves from their parents, just as they did when they were single. The message on the parents' answer machine says, "Call you later, Mom and Dad—we're going away for the weekend." After grandchildren are born, the young marrieds may call and ask, "Do you think you could come over and baby-sit Saturday night?" They may discover that their parents (us) actually know a thing or two, because we learned a lot from all the work we had to do raising our own children (them).

A Mix of Influences

We who have raised our children know that many factors influenced our relationships with our kids. Those of us with more than one child know that even such superficial thing s as looks and personality can make a difference. Some children, even from birth, are easier to get along with, and this feeds on itself. More people bill and coo at them, giving them more attention, which makes them still easier to get along with. And so it goes all through their lives.

Try as we might—and as reluctant as we are to admit it—we may not always treat our children equally. Unconsciously, parents have favorites: the outgoing child over the taciturn one; the better looking child over the plain one; the one who's most like us or most like what we'd like to be. Fathers may be more protective of their daughters; mothers may favor their sons. Needless to say, this favoritism, whether unwitting or intentional, can create stresses and strains.

Money relationships make a difference. Those of us who are prosperous can afford to help our children. If we do, though, an equal relationship between our kids and us isn't possible, particularly, as we'll see later, if they need our financial help. Even if we all would like our relationship to be equal, they remain dependent—and they know it.

Geography can take a toll. If our children live far enough away, frequent contact, casual socializing, and ordinary help with daily living isn't possible. If they live close by, we run the risk of having too much contact and familiarity.

The Echo Of Our Parents

How we were raised can have a significant influence on how we raise our children. "What goes around comes around," says Dr. Allan Entin, a clinical psychologist and a former president of the Family Psychology Division of the American Psychological Association. We may adopt our parents' methods, consciously or unconsciously. (Have you ever said something to your children, and with your inner ear heard yourself sounding exactly like your mother or father?)

If your family had a tradition of doing certain things in certain ways—celebrating holidays, for instance—you might continue the tradition. If your children want to follow suit, that's fine. If they resent or dislike the tradition, though, will you accept it as their choice and not a personal rejection?

After all, we reserve the right to reject the way our parents acted without necessarily rejecting them. If we weren't happy with the way we were brought up, we may have consciously decided, as many parents have, to deal with our kids totally differently. One father said, "My father was an autocratic, stern parent who demanded obedience and never seemed interested in his children as people. I've tried not to be that kind of parent." Another parent agreed: "My parents, especially my father, were demanding and critical, so I tried hard not to be such a parent."

On the other hand, how we raised our children can have a lasting effect on our relationship with them as adults. Being too laid back in reaction to our overly demanding parents, for example, can also have unhappy consequences. If, despite our best intentions, we didn't set appropriate boundaries, our children may never have learned how to handle difficulties or develop a strategies for making choices. Or, if our children were allowed to have their own way—after all, being the good guy is easier than saying no—they may have gone into the real world and discovered the hard way that others won't handle their problems for them. And if our children can't solve their problems or solve them poorly, they may blame us, their parents—especially if they have to live with unpleasant consequences—or turn to us for help that we may not be able or willing to give.

Will It Ever Be Equal?

Once our children are on their own, we may think we're on our way to an equal relationship in which there is no advantage-taking on either side. But, can this equality be realized? No, says Dr. Fine, and parents who aspire to this unrealistic goal will end up disappointed.

Here's the catch. Even adult children still view parents unconsciously as authority figures in the parent-child relationship. This has been the relationship since infancy, and it's very difficult if not impossible to change it. Adult children often think that parents are still there to satisfy their needs, just as they did in childhood.

When our children enter our homes, for instance, it's almost inevitable that they will regress to some of the old patterns. Some of the old feelings can reassert themselves. Equally unwittingly, we may take on the parental role again. *Are you hungry? Where's your sweater...it's cold outside.* (One successful psychologist, a man who fully understands this 'throwback' phenomenon, says it still happens to him when he visits his parents.)

Why do kids take advantage? The same reasons that we all take advantage. It's easier, it's more comfortable, it's been the typical pattern. (Women who've been in consciousness-raising groups already know about this—maybe some of us could use a consciousness-raising group for parents.)

Don't forget that some of our children were teenagers during the *don't-trust-anyone-over-30* era, which was followed by the *me-first* era. And we live in an era when marketers—

who are often the same ages as our children—promote a negative image of older people: we're afraid to try something new…we're losing some of our savvy…we keep to ourselves too much…we sit in our rocking chairs. (They deserve to lose a lot of sales for this. We don't fit this image, but we do resent being depicted this way. Wait till these marketers are our ages!)

Besides, our kids are human. They can be just as insensitive, selfish, and ignorant of other people's needs as anyone else can be.

Parents Are People Too

Our children may also forget—if they ever truly realized it—that our current jobs, hobbies, and recreational activities are very important to us. They may not recognize that the favor or help they are asking for is really an imposition on us. One mother says, "When our children call me and can't get me at home, they complain. That's good. They need to understand that we have our own lives to lead, and that's why it's hard to get hold of us. They forget that they're not there when we call."

(To be perfectly fair, some of us miss having to cook dinner for a family, or not having to go to work in the morning. We look to requests from our children for help to give us a purpose in life. We need to feel needed. This is our problem, one which we cannot blame on them.)

We also have our weaknesses. Though we may not admit it, parents want perfect kids, according to Dr. Thomas T.Olkowski, a psychologist in private practice in Denver. Any flaw poses a threat. If you were asked to list ten things you wanted from your kids, he asks, would you mention status? It wouldn't appear on the list, would it? But wouldn't it be there in reality? (If this were true confession time many of us would have to admit to this sin of pride.)

Sometimes we actually feed an unequal relationship by reminding our child, "If you had listened to me this wouldn't have happened." The closer this statement is to the truth, the worse it can be to say. Chances are the child wasn't in the right place or time or frame of mind to hear you or to take your good advice. *If you had listened to me* can be one of the most annoying concepts in any language. None of us needs to be reminded of past mistakes—we know about them only too well, because we have had to live with their consequences.

Old and often unresolved grievances can be major roadblocks to good relations. Sometimes parents and children get stuck reliving certain aspects of their past together, and this focus chains them to unproductive behavior.

Consider, for example, the Semple family. Madeline, the oldest daughter, had been a chubby child with few friends. This bothered her parents, particularly her mother, since it reminded her of her own fat and unhappy childhood. She nagged Madeline constantly about her eating habits—which indeed *were* terrible. Unfortunately Madeline heard the nagging about all aspects of their relationship, not just about food. In fact, she remembers this nagging as one constant in her relationship with her mother.

Madeline eventually went to work in a different city, changed her diet, and became a regular at a fitness club. She is now an attractive, well-built, plump young woman. Her mother saw the change, and came to understand the underlying cause for her nagging. She resolved never to discuss food with her daughter. Yet, Madeline's visits never go smoothly. If her mother ask an innocuous question about her social life or mentions a minor difference of opinion, Madeline's reacts with an anger and bitterness that she doesn't hesitate to voice. She's responding not to what's being asked, but to the unpleasant memories from her childhood.

Parents, too, can have resentments that come out in camouflaged ways. Excessive anger over minor issues, for example, may be a mask for other grievances, such as the child's consistent taking advantage of the parents or failure to offer help when it's needed. Why so much anger? It serves a hidden purpose, says Dr. Olkowski. Parents are afraid to reveal the true cause of their anger. They may keep hidden, even from themselves, that they think their child takes advantage of them or doesn't offer help when it's needed. They may fear that by speaking up they will challenge their child's love. It's easier to misplace the anger by becoming furious when a child forgets to call at a promised time or comes late to a family dinner. What's hidden or denied in relationships can undo everyone's attempt to achieve harmony.

Is there ever a perfect balance? Of course not. This is the real world, after all. Push comes to shove and shove comes to push, even when no one wants to push or shove in the first place. Imbalances exist, imbalances which plead to be remedied. It can be done, as we shall discover.

CHAPTER XII

Prime and Re-Prime Time

We must have done something right. Parents often have misgivings about how they'd raised their sons and daughters. But they have only compliments for how these same sons and daughters were raising their kids, the grandchildren. The younger generation "devote more time to their children"; they're "more patient," and "more relaxed." (And why not, considering the good start we gave them—the best education we could scarcely afford and lots of leeway in getting started in their careers.)

Gratifying though this is, it doesn't change our wish to have more balanced relationships with our progeny. Before we look into this, let's contemplate some facts of parental life. According to sociologists Alice and Peter Rossi, growing up in a happy family profoundly affects how adult children feel about their parents and how helpful the children will be to their aging parents. By contrast, it has much less effect on how parents feel about their adult children or how much help parents will give them.

Is that fair? Of course not! Most of us learned long ago that fairness was not a fact of family life. In fact, nature has conspired against us. Scientists have discovered a biochemical basis that influences all mammals, including humans, to pair into cooperative units and rear their young. Two hormones, *oxitocin* in females and *vasopressin* in males, impel men and women to bond, mothers to respond to babies, and children to connect to the outside world and make friends.

Humans are more complex than other mammals. Non-human mammals do not worry that their children won't learn how to swing from the branches, run fast enough to escape hunters, or find the right mate. Animal parents watch out for their babies up to a certain age. Then *It's your jungle out there, kids. Good luck, and goodbye.*

We do it differently. We do worry and we never say goodbye. But even our connections to our children change. To help us evaluate what's reasonable, and what isn't, let's take a look at what psychologists, sociologists, and academics say these connections should be.

Can The Relationship Be Equal?

Most experts doubt that we and our kids will ever look at each other eye to eye. There will always be an imbalance caused by the feelings of responsibility that parents have for children, a natural outcome of the many years when we actually were responsible for them. The scale has been heavily weighted on their side for too long. This doesn't mean that it can't be better balanced at this point in our lives—with everyone's needs respected and no one being taken advantage of. But an absolute equality may be beyond our reach. It may not even be appropriate.

Why do our children sometimes take advantage of us—and why do we permit it? Sometimes it just happens—we slide into the pattern without being aware of what's happening. It's often easier that way. Life is more comfortable if we continue to do what we've always done. Besides, we don't want to measure who is doing more for whom—we don't really care about that, and we are not looking for a scale that is perfectly balanced.

But why do we permit it when our better judgment tells us it's not good? There are many reasons, all of them understandable if not thoroughly valid. Some parents, according to

Philadelphia psychologist Elaine K. Hankin, want to make up for what was wrong when their children were young. *He wasn't good-looking; she was awkward; they were painfully shy.* The parents tried to compensate then—and they continue trying to do so now.

For others, it's guilt. Perhaps their jobs required them to work nights and weekends, so they didn't spend time with their children. Perhaps the home atmosphere was unpleasant because the parents continually fought. Maybe it was an unplanned pregnancy and the child was rejected initially. Or maybe there was a painful breakup of the marriage. Many of these parents try to assuage their guilt by being too generous, too permissive, too forgiving.

Some parents feel they have no alternative. A single mother says, "Friends say I shouldn't help my sons at all. But how can I leave them stranded, particularly when their father makes promises to them and doesn't come through?"

For some, it's that overworked phrase, 'low self-esteem.' They feel subconsciously that they're not worthy of a child's love. Then they fear they will lose the love if they change their ways. They are, says psychologist Donna Allender, afraid to be angry at their child and to do something that will make the child angry at them. Or else they're afraid that if they alienate the kids they won't get to see their grandchildren as often as they'd like—possibly that they'll be cut off entirely. So they continue to be unhappy doing what they've always done.

For still other parents, their children continue to give them a purpose in life. The time, effort, and money they spend on their children hides the emptiness in their own lives.

Regardless of the cause, the effect can be dissatisfaction and a strong wish for change. After all, a healthy relationship is reciprocal; it provides for the self-interest of everyone. When it doesn't, when there are major imbalances, hidden consequences result. Morris Shechtman, a former psycho-therapist who now consults on management problems, says,

"If you permit yourself to be taken advantage of, you will have to pay a price, and so will your child." As we have seen, the price for allowing your children to depend on you is just that—they continue to be dependent and don't learn to be mature, self-responsible adults.

The Unseen Danger of Generosity

There is another hazard, according to Shechtman. "If you give all the time, it becomes a family 'welfare system.' You've created an entitlement that can be demeaning to the recipient; an entitlement that can give rise to an unconscious need for 'revenge.' The recipients who get the most help will have the greatest need for revenge."

"Revenge" may seem like a rather strong word. Other psychologists describe the same reaction using milder terms like *retribution*, and *resentment*. Still, it explains the father who said, "The child I gave the most to is the one who is least grateful."

Allan Entin, a psychologist in Richmond, Virginia, says, "If you've been a 'do-fer' parent, and you're still at it, you're discouraging them from being 'do-fers' for themselves. In the long run, this is not helpful." For example, one mother, talking about her unemployed daughter, said, "I may have made life too easy for my children. If I had to send two children to college I would take any reasonable job available to help pay for their education and not wait for the 'perfect' job to come along."

The key question, Dr. Entin says, is: "Do you care enough *not* to rescue them?"

Starting To Make Changes

Problems are normal in families. If you have friends who claim that their family relationships are trouble-free take it with a grain of salt (or salt substitute). Many of them are kidding themselves, or they are in denial, or their definition of *problem* may be suitable for them but not for you. Virtually all families have problems, the essential differences being the severity of the problems and the ways in which families deal with them.

Let Elaine Hankin remind you that you did the best you could while you were raising your children. Do not become a hostage to guilt. The *mea culpa* (I am guilty) syndrome is more than self-defeating: it can harm those it's supposed to benefit. Hankin points out that the 'beneficiaries' of your guilt can find your help a cause for resentment or even a source of guilt for them. They know they have taken without reciprocating or without reciprocating on a reasonable scale.

Once you decide that you want more equality in your family relationship, you need to analyze what is standing in the way. Consider if you really want to make changes and if change is even possible. You may not answer in the affirmative. This may not be the right time for change, or the price may be too high. More on this later.

For the present, assume that you want to pursue change. Step back and try to be objective about what the issues really are. Put away the idea that there is a right and a wrong answer. Consider instead that you have a problem, a disagreement, an issue—call it what you will—that needs to be negotiated. The heart of negotiation is understanding the perspective of the individuals involved, seeing what can be be done to alleviate the situation, identifying the possible compromises, and finally coming to some agreement.

How you go about this will be very personal, depending on previous and existing family relationships, current arrangements, how important it is to make the changes, and who needs to do the changing. If your children have taken advantage of you only once, the need for change may not be that urgent. If they have done it frequently, the fault probably lies with you, not them. You must do the changing.

It takes a lot of work to change behavior patterns, particularly family patterns. This is never a win/lose question. It is a problem of incorrect expectations—on your part and theirs.

The first thing to do is to decide what do want your relationship with your children to be and how you think it should be different from the way it is today. You, the parent or parents, have to set your own bottom line—what kind of behavior will you consider unacceptable? Only you can decide how you want to be treated; only you can lay out the ground rules and abide by them.

A certain amount of indecision is going to be inevitable. Here's a typical situation—the mother who said, "My daughter and I are friends almost all the time, but I'm not always willing to lend her my car. Sometimes I resent it—then she resents my reluctance. She once said, 'If you want to say no, just say no.'" If you are feeling indecisive, remember that a straightforward answer is much easier to deal with—the person knows exactly where everyone stands and can act accordingly.

It is essential that parents operate as a team. Most families exhibit what psychologists call "role agreement." One parent may be the worrier who is sensitive to and cares for the emotional status of the children. For a variety of reasons—the demands of work, the different personalities involved, the sex of the child (girls may be more comfortable with their mothers, boys with their fathers)—the other parent may be less aware or less involved, though not less caring. Adult children, just like young children, can look for this edge, especially if they know from past experience that either Mom or Dad can't say *no*. Any decisions must be mutual and clear.

One inevitable consequence of making changes is that the others involved—your children and possibly your spouse—will have to change as well. Many of us resist changes precisely because, while we know what we want to do and are prepared to do, we aren't sure how others will react. Will they be angry? Will they resist? Will they refuse? These are frightening possibilities that can keep us from doing things differently. So it's important to be very clear on how vital it is to you to proceed, and, if you decide you must, to do so in the best way.

This may not be easy. But like so many things in life, it doesn't get any easier if it's postponed. Better sooner than later, because if you don't talk and continue to sacrifice, the patterns become more and more ingrained, and any change at all becomes much more difficult to accomplish.

Dealing With Problems

Parents have two main complaints: their offspring don't respect their parents' time, and they are careless about their financial dealings. We'll consider the latter complaint in a subsequent chapter. Here, let's look at baby-sitting as an example of parent-child difficulties. Babysitting involves both a complex mix of emotions and an actual, physical strain—it's hard to lift a 20-pound baby or chase after a two-year-old future Olympic runner.

The Whites had planned to go out to dinner on Saturday to celebrate the birthday of a close friend. They had already bought the gift and were looking forward to the evening. Two days before the dinner their daughter called—something had come up and they couldn't get a regular sitter on such short notice. Could the Whites please babysit on Saturday night?

The Browns were still employed but often would babysit on weekends for their lawyer-daughter and son-in-law. Occasionally their daughter would call to ask Mrs. Brown to sit on mornings when the regular sitter was sick. She had to be in court and, after all, "It's easy to get a substitute for you, but no one can take my place." Mrs. Brown was furious at this comment, but she usually swallowed her pride and babysat.

Then there's the Black family, who picked up their grandchildren from school several afternoons a week. It's not a chore they volunteered for—they did it because they were asked to. They actually enjoyed doing it, but it meant planning their schedule around the school year and foregoing activities that conflicted with the school calendar.

None of these parents was particularly pleased with this situation, but no one knew how how to change it. What did all of them have in common? They all said, in effect, that their lives were less important than the lives of their children. By accepting these obligations, they accepted standing in second place.

When parents do not respect their own status as autonomous individuals with their own lives to lead, two things happen. First, they lose the self-esteem which is important in any dealings with children or anyone else. As one mother in a family with adult stepchildren on both sides said, "My children don't take advantage of me because I don't let them! That is my choice. It would not be to my liking. But most of all it would lessen their respect for me and for themselves if they were allowed to take undue advantage. They have grown to be independent, caring adults partly because of this philosophy."

Second, parents can and do react inappropriately. Sometimes they acquiesce without a word when their children wouldn't have minded at all if they'd said no. At other times, they refuse reasonable requests simply because they are so resentful and frustrated. Perhaps they react with extreme anger or blow up over minor and non-related issues. Subconsciously they're still chafing at foregoing the dinner party or taking a day off from work.

The problem with these reactions is not only that they're inappropriate; they're also unclear. They baffle the children, who do not know what's expected of them or where they've overstepped the bounds. They may become confused, upset, and possibly resentful and frustrated. Dissension is reciprocated.

It is important to communicate what you want to your children in clear terms. Allan Entin emphasizes the importance of taking what he calls the "we position." Parents have to say both to themselves and to their kids: "We are our own persons; we cannot allow ourselves to be imposed on this way. We must speak up and say to our children, here is what you should expect. This is what we will/can do for you; this is what we won't/can't do for you. You cannot take us for granted. We'll let you know if we can do what you ask. We can't or won't go on just providing this service for you."

Elaine Hankin offers some further advice. If you feel that you're not strong enough or that this isn't the right time to take a strong stand, do an "incremental setting of limits." Start with minor controls—"I can't come at 1:00 o'clock, but I can come at 2:00." Then, you can work up to more emphatic limits—"I can't come this week, but I can come next week." Deciding what you want and then discussing it with your children is a much better, and in the long run, easier way.

Choosing the right time to communicate your needs is part of getting to a satisfactory solution, though it is not always a simple task to know exactly when the right time has arrived. It's certainly easier to identify the wrong time. It should not be when the grandchildren are there, when the young couple is on the way out the door for the evening's festivities, or when you are angry or tired. A better time will come or can be planned.

When that time comes, be loving and firm. You can say that "We parents are getting resentful because it feels like you've been taking us for granted. This situation has developed before any of us realized it. We don't want to be resentful. That's why it's important to discuss this and get a fresh start."

Can you send a letter or three as a substitute for a personal discussion? Opinions vary. Some authorities said it would simply be ducking the issue and wouldn't settle anything. Others said it was okay, at least to get the discussion started. It has this advantages—a written letter can be re-read and evaluated so that it sets the desired tone and says what you really want to say. Then you don't have to agonize *if only I had said...* Not incidentally, writing also helps to clarify your thoughts.

It is important that whatever you do be the right choice for you. For some people the right step could be getting professional help. For others, it might be a discussion with a member of their faith, a psychologist, or some other trained listener or counselor. They can hear things in a discussion that you can't—honest feelings of love and respect, for example, beneath the sometimes hostile words.

Achieving Your Objectives

How do you establish equilibrium? Practice, practice, practice, says Denver psychologist Thomas Olkowski. You have to work on it continually. If you want to change your relationship with your kids, he says, you have to pay attention to what is good in your relationship, the positive aspects that continue despite the dissention, frustration, and hurt. Focus on what really matters. Parents too often overlook the child's admirable core values or take them for granted. Kids also often focus on the things about parents that bug them and overlook their parents' virtues.

"We walk a straight line as a parent but can easily slip off," says educator Jerry Allender. "Perfect balance is impossible. But honesty doesn't mean saying it all. Spare me too much honesty—saying it all can be hurtful." There is a difference between the honesty of being connected to somone and the honesty of pointing out someone's faults. (Telling faults under the guise of honesty is more like putting in the knife and turning it.)

If you don't mind helping your children but do mind a lack of appreciation, think about this, says Dr. Mark Fine, current editor of *Family Relations Journal*. Maybe your kids appreciate you more than you realize but don't say it. In general, people don't say good things, give compliments, or show appreciation to authority figures—and to our children we are authority figures. There's a subconscious feeling that people in authority don't need appreciation because they are powerful. This 'authorities-don't-need-it' attitude has its roots in childhood, but it can carry over well into adulthood.

Never overlook the power of an apology, either. As one mother told me: "No woulda, shoulda, coulda—no going back and doing things over. But, one can learn from a mistake. First, tell your children, 'I wish I had understood better, I wish I had not made it so difficult, and I hope you realize I did the best I could.' Then follow up by really listening to their feelings. This can help heal a past hurt."

Psychologist, columnist, and talk-show host Dan Gottlieb agrees. He remembers having a patient tell him that she was hurt when he quoted her in one of his columns (though not by name). When he said he was sorry he'd hurt her, she started to cry, then explained that no one, in her long years of difficulties, had ever said he was sorry. The apology not only released tears, it also alleviated a deep pain.

Who is the parent who hasn't wounded his or her children while they were growing up? Who hasn't been wounded by a child? And who, on either side of the parent/child seesaw, wouldn't be healed by the words *I'm sorry*.

What-If

What if the source of misunderstanding is one child's belief that a sibling is being favored? Because children and the paths their lives follow are so different, we have to treat them differently. Fairness isn't the always the question that need is. A good way to handle this, says Dr. Fine, is to explain to the 'cheated' child your rationale for what you are doing. But, you don't have to justify or defend your actions. You don't *owe* your kids an explanation.

What if you don't see any way of really changing things? You can't bring yourself to discuss it...it's too touchy...business is bad...your son or daughter is in the throes of a divorce...has lost a job. This is not the time to add burdens on top of burdens. Postpone the discussion until a more propitious time. There is always the possibility that the problem will work itself out in the interim.

What if you believe you simply can't have an honest and fruitful discussion with your children, but it is important that you remain a family? It may be time to re-evaluate where your stand, to focus on what's going well. Does the good outweigh the bad? In most cases, it does. If so, write off the bad and enjoy the good.

Suppose you had a bad financial debt and you saw no way to collect. You would probably chalk it up to experience and wait for a different time to recoup your losses. Or you would simply wrap it up, throw it away, and forget about it. Why not do the same with an emotional debt as well? Learn from the experience and forget it. The whole family will benefit.

CHAPTER XIII

Dollar$ and Sen$e

There is another name for parents: safety net, or, to be more specific, financial safety net.

We know, and our children know, that if they face a financial crisis and look as if they might fall, we'll be there to keep them from falling or to catch them, if that's what's needed. But we sincerely and fervently hope—and so do they—that the safety net will be unnecessary. We're at the time in our lives where we want to admire their independence and cherish our own.

Do we mind? We don't. Some thirty to forty years ago, according to financial planners, it was almost a disgrace to have to borrow money from your parents. Now it's an accepted practice and another example of how times have changed. Our parents often had a difficult time establishing themselves. They weren't in a position to offer much financial help, didn't have the benefits some of us have (particularly Medicare), and were more likely to be in ill health. But they still helped us achieve our present wealthier, healthier, and more secure status. They'd certainly approve our safety net philosophy.

There's one dilemma, however. If we do give or lend, we want to be sure that we don't bring down on our unwitting heads the "Law of Unintended Consequences." Sometimes, the money we give or lend works well. But at other times, despite our good intentions, it proves to be, at best, a mixed blessing and, at worst, a disaster. The trick is to know when it is blessed to give and when it is blessed to refrain from giving or to offer something else.

Money's Other Face

To understand why this is so, we need to take a look at what money really is.

We remember from Economics 101 that money is what is know as a *medium of exchange*. We use it to pay our bills, leaving, we hope, enough for us to live it up a little. Money is also exchanged for nonmaterial things. Money is power, for example. Those with money have power—for themselves and over others. Those without money must acquire it or remain dependent or powerless. (This is one of the important lessons of the women's movement, by the way) It's been this way for a long time. Almost 2,000 years ago the Roman philosopher Ovid said, "So long as he is rich even a barbarian is attractive." To which Shakespeare added, "If money go before, all ways lie open."

Outside of economics textbooks, however, money is not just a medium of exchange. It's also a medium for revealing our unconscious selves, showing some of our hidden needs and wants, or telling the world that we have made it without necessarily revealing how much we have made.

People are funny about money. We can get all kinds of information about money for the price of a phone call, a postcard, a magazine subscription. We can get expert advice on balancing budgets, buying a house, investing, writing a will. And we do make the calls, read the articles, and get the advice; then we go and do otherwise. Why? Because our ears are tuned to our internal adviser who tells us something different. This advice often is so attuned to our emotional needs that, against our informed judgments, we follow our inner adviser. If you ever wonder why your children, your spouse, or even you do what you do with money—this may explain it.

When we talk about money with our adult children we're also talking about power, unconscious motivations, fears and desires. When our children ask for loans, they're not only putting on the line their finances but also much of their independence, self-esteem, and status. And when we give or lend them money we're reinforcing our views of ourselves, and—though we don't think of it this way—our independence, self-esteem, and status.

Not that money is a frequent topic of family conversation—unless it's other people's money. Discussion of our money is one of the last taboos in our society. (If you doubt this, try leaning across the table at a dinner party and asking someone, "How much money do you make?" or "How much are you worth?"). Why the taboo? Because money is associated with status. "In America," said three quarters of the respondents to a survey of middle-class young people, "money is how we keep score."

Family Money Is Different

Money has a special meaning within the family, because people in families have special relationships with each other. The sociologist Marcia Millman puts it this way: "Family money is viewed as a special kind of money, and it takes on many symbolic meanings beyond its actual cash value." There are undercurrents in family money matters that we, and our children, may not be aware of. Money is, in Millman's words, "tangled up" with love and perceptions about how we've been dealt with in the family.

There have also been major changes outside the family. Men's and women's roles have been altered considerably, not simply by families' need for two incomes to maintain standards of living, but also by changes in society, such as those brought about by the feminist movement. With these changes, people's perceptions of their roles in society and society's perception of them as individuals haven't always lined up neatly. The stressful and distressful need for each of us to reorient our ideas about our places in society has been compared, by some sociologists, to deprogramming someone who has been in a cult.

Part of the stress for men has been their historic role as the good provider. Theoretically, this is no longer their responsibility alone. In the day-to-day world, however, wives' incomes are still considered supplementary, men are still defined by what they do, and men who ask for leaves of absence for child care are still considered less-promotable. When a son has to ask for a loan, he may feel he's failed as this so-called good provider, particularly if his father did well.

Not that it's easy for women either. They're caught in cross-currents—there are still people who disapprove when mothers with babies choose to work outside the home (*They should stay home until the kids go to school—harrumph*) and people who disapprove when they stay home (*They should give their husbands a hand—harrumph*).

These attitudes may be changing, but the world still expects men to be the main provider. You'll know these attitudes have really changed when there's a men's magazine titled *Working Father* and women's magazines have articles titled, "How To Cope When He Makes More Than You Do."

There's another complication: our sons and daughters may feel ambivalent about accepting our help. After all, they were accustomed to getting money from us in their younger days. If we offer it, accepting our help may seem like the thing to do. And it may cause discomfort, especially if we let them know that we don't approve of how they're spending the money by asking questions like "Did you have to buy a big car?" or, "You're taking a vacation now?" If they've accepted the money, they may not talk back or defend their choices, but secretly they could be angry or resentful of our criticism.

Even if we give without any judgments or conditions, our kids still may feel guilty. As one young woman said, "My parents give me no reason to feel they attach strings to their dollars, but I'm dismayed at the nauseatingly sweet way I thank them…and in the greedy way I sometimes secretly wish the check had been for more."

Mixing families and money is never easy, especially because of the hidden buttons we push. We're dealing with very complicated emotions that are sometimes expressed financially. "Money," says one psychiatrist, "is one of the common places where emotional issues hitchhike." And this is true both for parents and children.

Questions For Parents

Should you or should you not lend or give money to your children? There are a few questions you should ask yourself before you make your decision. Remember that you're putting at risk something more important than money. You are also risking family relationships—and you can't put a price on those.

Of course your intentions are to do what's best for your children. But sometimes your heart takes precedence over your head. And sometimes your feelings about what's best for your children take precedence over your better judgment. Perhaps you want to make up to a child for some neglect in the past; perhaps you think your child isn't living properly and you can point the way to an improvement; perhaps your child is faltering and you know how to correct mistakes. Money will accomplish these goals—you think. You could be wrong.

Can Loans Overcome Long-standing Family Tensions? When her daughter Ann was young, Vera Allen had to spend more time with Ann's invalid brother. Ann grew up feeling neglected and unloved. She spurned college, had a childless marriage, lived poorly despite financial help from her parents, and divorced after ten years.

Ann's second marriage started lavishly—$1,000 dresses, a mink coat, foreign cars—but no savings account. Then came the recession. Ann and her husband borrowed $60,000 from Vera. Now they're successful again, but they've made no move to repay the borrowed money.

When they unexpectedly inherited some money, Mrs. Allen suggested that they invest it in their name, but give her the interest to repay their loans. Their response was to say that "We'd like to, but we have credit card bills to pay." Mrs. Allen has reluctantly realized that keeping the loans is Ann's way of compensating herself for the neglect she felt as a child and that Ann doesn't believe she really owes any money.

Would they be better off, Mrs. Allen wonders, if they had talked about the anger between them? It would have been painful, but would it have been any less painful than Ann's belief that her mother never truly loved her? Are they a family only as long as Vera is their banker? If she tries to collect, will their relationship end? She's asked her daughter to have lunch and discuss their finances, but for months Ann hasn't been able to find the time. These questions weigh heavily on Mrs. Allen's mind as she waits for that long-postponed lunch.

Can Financial Support Induce Children To Adopt Your Lifestyle And Values? The Jones' family urged their daughter and her family to move nearer to them because, they said, the climate was healthier and they could get to know their grandchildren better. But there was another motive that led them to overstate the job situation in their area. The Jones disapproved of their daughter's lifestyle; what to her was casual to them was "unclean and unhealthy."

The Joneses paid for the long-distance move with part of the money they had set aside for their retirement. They didn't expect to be repaid, but they did expect the young family to keep house their parent's way, to take any jobs until they found better ones, to visit often, and to help their parents with errands and chores.

It didn't work. Mother and daughter renewed their old conflicts; mother tried to dominate while daughter resisted. The children, sensing the tensions, showed signs of stress. Daughter and son-in-law weren't willing to take jobs they felt were beneath their dignity. They needed additional financial help, but they resented both the attempts to change their lifestyle and the subtle reminders that they should be grateful for being rescued.

Finally, the painful time came when the parents had to say they could no longer afford to help. There was a very noticeable chill. Communication became a one-way street from parents to children. Now weeks go by without visits or phone calls...unless the parents are needed for babysitting.

The Jones are both hurt and angry. They say they'd like to "show them an itemized bill for the thousands of dollars they've spent," but of course they won't. They ask themselves why they ever got involved in their children's lives and wish now that they hadn't. They penny-pinch to replace the retirement money they spent and resent the fact that they have to. Their biggest regret is that they don't see their grandchildren very often. Instead of drawing this family together, money became a wedge that drove them apart.

Can Money Solve Children's Personal And Career Problems?
Richard Brown was a lawyer who was as disorganized as he was bright. During good times when the demand for lawyers was high, he practiced as an independent attorney with the help of a partner who kept after him, supplemented by regular gifts of money from his parents, Al and Martina Brown. But when the market got tight, his partner pulled out, leaving Richard on his own. Al Brown continued making regular deposits into Richard's bank account, increasing the amount to compensate for the loss of Richard's partner.

Richard went through several clients who were annoyed by his careless work habits. He took several full-time jobs, some part-time jobs, and then went through a period of unemployment. This put a strain on his marriage, which eventually broke up over the stress. By the time he recognized he had to reform, Richard was in his forties, with a spotty resume and few contacts. He is now unemployed, and his job prospects only get dimmer and dimmer. Al Brown wonders: without the help from home would he have gotten his act together while it still would have done some good?

If there is a moral to these stories, it is this: lending money doesn't solve old family grievances, entitle parents to try to manage their children's lives, or correct children's shortcomings. Money often does nothing more than paper over old problems or postpone decisions, sometimes beyond the time when constructive change is possible.

Money Well Lent

Money does not buy happiness. It does not cure all ills. It cannot turn the sow's ear into the silk purse. (Unwisely used, though, it can turn the silk purse into the sow's ear.) Unrealistic expectations can only lead to disappointment.

When we provide appropriate financial help to our kids, we are really making an investment in our children's and grandchildren's lives. There may be no better investment we can make.

For examples, consider the following:

Jean and Martin's daughter and her husband had one baby already, wanted another, and couldn't sell their one-bedroom condominium. The parents on both sides were happy to lend them the down payment on a three-bedroom house with a big yard. The couple both have good jobs and, though there are no formal papers, they plan to repay the loan from their more-than-sufficient incomes.

The Washington's daughter, Claire, is a talented comedienne but needs time to make a name for herself. Her parents are more than glad to pay her rent until she becomes a star. It is their way of contributing to their daughter's future.

Rose's grandson has the potential to be a great doctor, but business is bad and his parents can only afford a mid-level college. She's happy to pay part of his tuition so he can go to a top-notch college with a highly regarded pre-med curriculum.

Call these 'living well' wills. Instead of being remembered after they're gone, these parents enjoy seeing their money enhance their children's lives right now. Everyone benefits. A deserving child gets some needed help; loving parents are able to see their help put to good use; and a family becomes even stronger. Everyone is happy. Unless...

When Is A Loan Not A Loan?

Many parents may say: *It wasn't a loan...unless they don't need the money any more* or *We don't expect the money will be returned...unless they can afford to pay it back.* To themselves, parents may be saying something quite different. When pressed, they may say: *It was a loan, but we (or I) don't count on getting it back...unless we need it, that is.*

Is it a loan, or is it a gift? What is meant by "unless they don't need it anymore?" or "unless they can afford to pay it back?" Who defines what a real need is or when someone can pay something back?

Imagine these parents going to their children and saying "Remember that money we lent you five years ago? Well, now we'd like to have it back." Unless there is a dire emergency, it's not likely they would do this. But any number of less-than-dire emergencies can make that loaned money seem quite desirable. Put yourself in the place of these parents.

- ✧ Just when you'd like to some make major plumbing re-pairs, your son or daughter arranges for expensive braces for a child with crooked teeth. Should you post-pone the plumbing or ask for the money back?
- ✧ Your car has been giving you trouble, and you'd like to buy a new one. Your son's mother-in-law can no longer live alone, so her children commit themselves to sharing the substantial cost of a continuing care com-munity. Would you say "Send me the money back, be-cause I need it more?"

Is it a loan or is it a gift? You had better be clear in your own minds. If it is a loan, then make it clear that you expect to be paid back. If it is a gift, even if you don't want to call it that, accept in your own mind that you are not expecting to have the money returned.

It would be wonderful if you could tell the future when you commit yourself to making a gift or a loan. But you can't, so you need to be very clear about what you are doing. Of course you trust your children, but how about their spouses? Are you sure that the marriage will last? Are you sure your situations won't change? Remember that your first responsibility is to yourself and the first maxim of parent-child money transactions must be never to jeopardize your own financial safety.

You do everyone a favor if you do not allow lending or giving money to become the source of continuing arguments between you and your partner. Don't poison the relationship between the two of you or make your children feel guilty or sad that they caused trouble. So both of you should agree, specifically, on how much you can sensibly afford to lend or give, when it should be done, and, if it's a loan, what the terms should be.

Once you have this settled, your next step is to evaluate the best way to give or lend money. This is the subject of the next two chapters.

CHAPTER XIV

The Joys And Agonies Of Giving

You've seen the bumper sticker: *We're Spending Our Children's Inheritance.* It gets laughs—but it's not necessarily true. The way many parents 'spend' their kids' inheritance…is on their kids.

If you're in a position to help your children, enjoy the feeling—especially if you still remember the anxieties you felt in the early days of your marriage. Would your money run out before the month did? Would the car last until you made the last payment? Would the baby's crib fit in your tiny bedroom until you could afford a bigger apartment? Leaving them an inheritance is not much on your mind; being able to help them now is. You'd like to spare them some of the worries you had—and why not? Like your parents before you, it's one of the reasons you've worked so hard.

The real estate industry certainly appreciates it. One of the most frequent gifts from parents to children is the down-payment on a house. It has undoubtedly saved the housing market from an even worse recession than it has had. The real estate industry owes us a special *Most-Reliable-Bankers-Over-The-Years* award.

The down-payment is one gift or loan that arouses few emotional hassles for parents—probably because we can literally see where the money has gone. We enjoy the feeling that we've helped start our kids on the path to prosperity and stability. This is true for those of us who gave our children a gift toward buying a house as well as those who lent money to buy a house even while we really meant it to be a gift which would never be repaid.

However, using money to help children is not without ambiguity and complication. Should we give or should we lend? Either or both? When? How much? Under what circumstances?

The Un-Romantic Kiss

There are no one-size-fits-all gifts or loans of money to family members, just as there are no-one-size-fits-all-clothes. In clothing it's one-size mis-fits just about everybody; in families all of us cut our own cloth to fit our own patterns, lumps and all. Interestingly enough, more parents are actually bothered that their children take advantage of their time than their money.

There is one platinum rule of parent-to-child gifts, though. It's the KISS principle: *Knowledgeable Individuals Stay Solvent*. Put differently, never give or lend money you can't afford to kiss goodbye. This is particularly important for older women who've been out of the job market for part of their lives, have traditionally earned less than men, have smaller pensions, and have invested more conservatively. Typically, they live longer and have a higher risk of outliving their retirement income.

Gifted Children

Giving, especially giving money, is a popular choice among parents—though there are many different reasons for doing it. For some parents, there's not even a question. As one couple said, "When there was a need we've given money—as much as we could without affecting our lifestyle. Why not see their lives made easier? You can't alter the reading of your own will."

For others, giving has been a way out of a difficult situation, especially for parents who have lent money and not been repaid in full or even in part. Some parents don't mind and make a gift of the debt simply by forgetting it. Some feel they've been taken advantage of. Still others are like the mother who said, "For the past 20 years I have only made outright gifts" to spare herself the irritation.

Giving money is not without side effects. Some parents gave happily, only to be annoyed or even angered when the money was spent in a way different from what they'd anticipated. Instead of being used, say, to replace shabby furniture, it was used to buy expensive toys which were played with briefly and then crammed into a closet already bulging with toys. Or it was spent on a skiing vacation in Switzerland (where a cup of coffee, with no refills, was $3, and a cheese fondue lunch for two was $37.50) instead of being deposited into the almost-empty savings account.

It's particularly (and understandably) irritating for parents who have assets, because they've been thrifty, to see their gifts spent in ways they consider spend-thrifty. It's also irritating when the parents suggest how the money should be spent only to find their suggestions ignored. This can happen for several reasons.

On the one hand, children's priorities are different from those of their parents. A young couple's hectic, two-career schedule may make them feel more like quarreling room-mates than a loving duo. They may believe their marriage is at risk (they may be right) and that they need time away from home to pull it together.

On the other hand, they may have heard the parent's suggestions very clearly and believed (maybe correctly) that their parents were trying to control their lives. Consciously or unconsciously, they may have chosen to ignore the suggestions to demonstrate their independence.

The Devil's Advocate

Our children's priorities may indeed be different. They will be wrong, or foolish, or inconsistent, or shortsighted, or all of the above. We may truly know better. Our kids may not want to follow our advice, simply because it is our advice. There have always been generation gaps, cultural gaps, and just plain divergences of lifestyles. Can parents induce or make their children change?

It is not likely, unless the children ask for advice and then follow it—assuming, of course, that we parents even know what to tell them. Not many parents want to be put in the position of having to offer incontrovertible evidence that they know what's best or that their children are wrong. It is we parents who must choose: either change our gift-giving practices and expectations or accept the situation as it is.

So, if you find yourself in this situation, allow yourself the luxury of griping to each other and to your friends. By all means remind yourself that your kids grew up during a time when spending and self-indulgence was the norm and when everybody simply expected to go now and pay later. Then, unless it really bothers you, do what so many other parents have done—live with the situation and continue making the gifts. After all, you've spent money on other activities that didn't bring you nearly as much enjoyment as seeing your kids enjoy your gifts.

To continue as the Devil's advocate, some children truly do have reason to be resentful—parents may be reminding them, more often than they (the parents) realize, that they (the children) are the beneficiaries of parental generosity. We all know parents who not only remind their children that they made the kitchen remodeling possible but also remark, when dinner is served, "These dishes we gave you certainly look nice on the table."

Psychologists might say that these parents are worrying that their children don't really love them and that they are hoping these reminders will make their children feel differently. Of course, it doesn't work that way. No one wants to be feel continually obligated.

There is nothing to keep children from refusing the gifts if they feel the price is too high. And children, too, probably indulge in some griping to each other and to their friends.

But the truth is more likely to be that they believe their parents can afford the gifts and, as a result, they don't turn them down. In their study of the exchange of help between parents and children, sociologists Alice and Peter H. Rossi point out that parents can recognize the difference between what their children need and what they can afford, while children seem to know about how much their parents can afford to give them.

There's another side to a refusal—most parents would be truly hurt. At best, such a refusal would be ungracious; at worst, it would be insulting. So children too have to accept their parents as they are—though it takes a rare degree of sensitivity and maturity for children to understand the emotional needs of their parents.

Parental Alternatives

If you are uncomfortable giving money for whatever reason, there are several things you can do—none of them perfect. You can, as suggested above, simply accept the situation. Some parents who did this have told me how pleased they were when, as their children got older, they began to appreciate what their parents had done and to admire them for it. Perhaps they haven't come out and expressed their gratitude—parents are still the authority figures who don't need gratitude—but they have shown it in other ways: invitations, phone calls, helping when parents were sick, sending books that would interest parents, finding dates for single parents, or bragging about their parents to their friends. Our kids may not always thank us in the ways we expect them to.

Not everyone can accept this, however. What if you really are not comfortable giving any more than the usual holiday and birthday presents, especially when you think the money you have given is being misspent? What if you want to give, but you also want to influence what the money is spent for? You do have alternatives.

There are ways of helping your children without giving outright gifts of cash. You can, for example, offer to pay school tuition for your grandchildren. (You may be surprised to find that nursery school costs as much today as it cost you to send your kids to college.)

Or, you can open a savings account in their names and contribute to it by means of small, automatic withdrawals from your bank. You can open a mutual fund account in their names and have small monthly sums automatically transferred from your bank. (Some mutual funds require initial investment as low as a hundred dollars, although one to several thousand dollars is more typical.) You won't miss the money (we hope) and they will learn how small regular savings and/or investments have long-run benefits.

You can offer to buy a service for them, such as a regular monthly gardener or a housecleaning service. (Just make it clear that you aren't criticizing their current gardening or housekeeping but that you are trying to spare them the heavy cleaning chores!)

While your children will certainly appreciate these gifts, there may be times when they would really rather have the money. That's not your concern—this was your decision and for you it was the best decision. (You may think—and you may be right—that it was the best decision for them too, but don't tell them that. Some things are much better left unsaid.)

Difficult But Necessary Choices

Some parents face a more serious question and a bigger problem: their children are careless about money, extravagant (though they may not think so) and/or terrible money managers. Some over-use their credit cards. Others go into debt and then count on their parents to bail them out. For these parents, even when they can afford to do so, money gifts are counterproductive, working at cross-purposes to what is best in the long run.

If this describes your kids, what can you do? Can you influence their choices or change their minds? Perhaps you can; perhaps you can't. But you can be responsible only for your own choices, those that are under your control. Once you've done the best you can do for your children according to your own judgment, you can do no more. You cannot make their choices, for you cannot be responsible for the choices they make. A checkbook has power, but it is not a magic wand. You need to accept that there are some things you cannot change.

Unhappily, there are times when parents must recognize that their children are making unreasonable requests and that the only intelligent answer is a refusal. This is not an easy thing to do. You risk antagonizing your children. There is always a chance that they will retaliate by ending your relationship—at least for a while. It's a fearful price to pay, but it is sometimes unavoidable.

The Brickers were put in this position when their son John wanted to abandon his job and go to London to become a playwright. He thought the atmosphere and the leisure would give him the inspiration and the time he needed. He asked them to finance him. They refused. He had already dabbled unsuccessfully in several careers with money borrowed from them, and he had not been able to pay any of it back.

They suggested instead that he start writing the play during nights and weekends, see how it went, and then consider the move abroad. John became angry and accused them of not appreciating the arts. He sold all his belongings to finance the trip. It would be nice, he thought, and theatrical to boot, to write a hit play and come home in triumph. But he didn't. He came home after a year, broke, ill, and without a play. They took him in. Instead of saying "We told you so," the Brickers helped him start a new career in computers.

You can only help your children as far as they are willing to be helped. Sometimes they must learn the hard way. Finances which are not in good order may reflect other problems in their lives. As we have seen, spending money can be a means of expressing or denying stresses or psychological hangups. You can't solve these either. If you think it would help, you might offer to pay for a therapist—but be diplomatic. With this offer, you are telling them that you think they need therapy, a suggestion that many people find threatening.

Sometimes, the best we can do is let them know that we're there for them if they need us. But help doesn't have to be financial, especially when financial help serves simply to continue their dependency. You may feel guilty, but guilt isn't necessarily appropriate. Saying *no* may be the most appropriate thing you can do. As psychotherapist Nathaniel Branden reminds us, "Parents imagine they possess a power no human being possesses: to determine what choices another person will make. If children need to learn where they end and their parents begin, parents need to learn the same lesson." Taking Branden's advice may help to level the field so that everyone, parents and children alike, can take responsibility for themselves.

Lending As An Option

Are loans the answer? Many parents don't think so. One parent, an anthropologist, spoke out against loans as a form of help, particularly when the children ask for the money. Having to ask, he believes, "corrupts the parent-child relationship." The children's very awareness of the debt, he said, could bias their behavior. They may become more aware of not doing something which will annoy parents, just as employees, dependent on their boss, won't do something that would aggravate the boss.

Children, this parent said, should, and probably do, behave in ways they expect their parents to approve. But this behavior should be based on a mutuality of love and respect, not dependency or debt.

Few would disagree with this or with the idea that it is a good thing to anticipate a child's needs and to give without being asked when a real need exists.

Still, there are times when a loan is preferable or more feasible, and times when it is the only possibility. This is the subject of the next chapter.

CHAPTER XV

Winning At Lending

Creditors have better memories than debtors.

We don't need Ben Franklin to remind us of that. Parents who are creditors are no different. They may not be as hard-nosed when it comes to repayment, but they do want good memories when they lend money to their children. So, when they agree to become their own children's bankers, they want to know the best way to proceed. Financial planners will tell them right away that they should have a written agreement spelling out all the terms. And they're right. That's the correct, business-like way to do it.

Yet most families don't do it this way for one very good reason. It isn't a business transaction. It's a family transaction. There's a world of difference.

Businesses put everything in writing because their transactions are based on distrust. It is not that the people involved are necessarily untrustworthy (though some of them might be), but because situations change. The people they trust and deal with today may not be the same people they will deal with tomorrow, next week, next year. A business doing well today may do poorly tomorrow. So business people provide for the future.

In a business deal, if your money isn't repaid, the problem is usually only the repayment. Why it wasn't repaid is not generally your personal problem. But when your children have problems, they become your problems. As one parent said, "When your children hurt, you hurt." When it's a business loan you have alternatives: you can sue, file a claim, evict. You don't really have these alternatives with your children. Even if you're angry with them, you don't want to hurt them. You can be nasty if necessary in a business deal. You can embarrass the people involved, show how foolish or stupid they were to get in the position they're in. You don't do that with your family.

Families are different because of trust. If your children say they're going to pay you back, would you really say to them, "I don't trust you?" It is not a question of trust. You do trust their intentions to pay you back. What you may not trust is their ability to repay and/or their ability to manage their financial affairs well enough.

Family deals do share one thing with business deals, though—uncertainty. Even if you have the utmost confidence in your children and their ability to repay, no one can foresee the future. The last thing you want is to see your children become part of the 'sandwich generation,' financially squeezed between helping you and providing for their own families. That's why the KISS principle (you can afford to kiss the money goodbye) is so vital.

Nor does the financial planner's legal document guarantee payment, especially where families are concerned. Children's lives shift and the legality of a document doesn't always make a difference. In one family, for example, the older daughter borrowed a large sum to make a down payment on a home, signed a legal document, and recently finished repaying the loan. But the younger daughter had two "terrible marriages and always needed money." Her parents lent her money so she wouldn't be dispossessed from her home and got the same legal documents. Still, she's never repaid the loan, legal document notwithstanding.

This illustrates one of the practical limits of legal documents. Their purpose is to insure payment, and in theory they are legally enforceable. But even in business, a legal document is not a guarantee. Its force depends on what happens in the future, and no one can guarantee that. More than a few businesses have found that the only use for their stacks of legal documents was as recycling fodder or ticker tape confetti when their debtors declared bankruptcy or failed outright.

The Advantages of Documents

There are times, however, when legal documents in a family serve some very important purposes. Some children prefer a document. It provides a business-like background to a loan. It focuses their thinking on how they can pay the loan back, and this, in turn, forces them to evaluate their finances. For many, it is a matter of pride to live up to the terms of the loan and offer proof that they have really come of age.

Consider Suzanne, a young public relations executive who wanted to borrow from her mother to finance a car. Her mother said she'd give her half the amount she needed—and require her to sign a loan agreement for the remainder. She emphasized it was a business transaction and that Suzanne should treat it as such. Then she wrote an informal agreement specifying the amount of the loan and the payment terms. Suzanne met the payments on time. She says now that "it was a good idea" and that she's glad her mother did it that way. It improved her budgeting prowess, she says. Suzanne is "proud" that she lived up to her obligation and thinks that other parents should follow the pattern her mother set.

If you think this is a good idea you don't need to create a form. Stationery stores sell several kinds of preprinted forms—demand promissory notes, time promissory notes, and time installment notes. They're written in plain English and cover the customary terms of loan agreements—the amount owed, how it is to be repaid (installments or lump sum), the time of payment, the rate of interest, plus more contingencies than you could ever hope to think of.

A document also reassures other members of the family. What if you have more than one child but are only lending to one? The documentation of the loan, with its commitment to the terms and its promise to repay, can ease the potential jealousy of the other children, even if they don't want or need a loan. It's a sign that you are expecting financial responsibility from your children and are not playing favorites. If need be, you can even insert a clause in your will reducing any child's final inheritance by any unpaid loan amounts. This will ensure that inheritances are equal, although you will have to record both the loan and the revised will if you want to give them legal force.

Guilt and the Green-eyed Monster

The world is not equal, and neither are your children—so should you, or can you, treat all your children equally? Many parents think not and give more to the needier child. They often feeling guilty while doing it, and worry about the jealousy that might result. This is a legitimate worry. Complaints that "He's the favorite child" or "You love her more than you love me" may be unavoidable, even if they are not true. Jealousy can extend even beyond the grave. Children have been known to argue bitterly over pieces of furniture their parents left, pieces that had no intrinsic value, simply because inheriting them symbolically compensated a child for perceived parental favoritism.

There is no perfect solution to the bite or even nibble of the green-eyed monster. Nevertheless, you are the best judge of what's right—and what's right doesn't necessarily include revealing things like who got what or how much. These things may often be guessed or revealed inadvertently. You still don't owe your children an explanation although you might want to give them one. If you are comfortable giving your reasons, by all means do so. Your children will value the respect you showed for them and their judgments.

One single mother, for example, had two very different children, both of whom she tried to treat appropriately but equally. She helped her son with gifts and loans while he and his wife were getting established. Alas, the two of them never managed well, and she "didn't think they ever would—but that's their problem." When she felt she'd done enough she told them that she expected to retire in a few years and would not be able to do any more. Her daughter, by contrast, had always been savvy, never needed help, and was already putting aside money for her children's college education. Nevertheless, the mother gave her major gifts at Christmastime in an attempt to make things equal.

On the other hand, a widower father, planning to remarry and move into a new house with his new wife, gave one of his daughters his old house. He explained his reasoning to his two other children. They held stable, professional, high-paying jobs, while their sister and her husband had low-paying civil service jobs and weren't likely to achieve as the other two had. He felt he was right, and made no apologies.

In each case, the parents shared their thoughts and reasons openly with all their children. They may not have opened the champagne in celebration, but the kids appreciated their parents' straightforward approaches. The families remained as close as ever.

Arm's Length Lending

Financial planners also recommend keeping parent-to-child loans at an 'arm's length' when possible. Let someone else, such as a bank, a credit union, or a brokerage company, be the lender. Your role will be the guarantor, providing the necessary collateral, such as stocks, bonds, or mutual funds, as security for the loan.

One of the advantages of this arrangement is the privacy of the financial information that the bank requires: the borrower's credit record, current debts, and ability to repay. Your offspring may be just as happy not to have you scrutinize these details—and you may be just as happy not to know, as long as they can repay the loan.

There are other benefits to this arrangement. There can be a natural tendency, when money is owed to a parent, for children to be a little lax about the payment dates. It is difficult enough to remind a friend or a colleague that they owe you money. It is much more difficult to call your children and say, "By the way, you promised to pay us on the first of the month, and here it is the middle of the month, and we haven't received your check." It can be embarrassing and breed resentment on both sides. The fact that they have indeed missed a payment makes it even more touchy, since they are likely to feel guilty.

It is often better to be out of the picture. The bank will work out a feasible repayment schedule and require your children to analyze their finances. Meanwhile, they will build their credit ratings, and you will keep your assets.

Some parents have been pleased to trust their children to pay back loans at more or less regular intervals. But, what happens if the payments stop coming? Should you remind them there's money due—and give them a deadline? When this happened to the Wallers—"Our youngest didn't want to talk about it"—they hated the thought of giving her a deadline. Should they have forgotten it? Many parents, including the Wallers, have done just that. This may not be a happy solution, since it encourages a casual attitude toward parents' loans and parents' money in general.

If you can't afford to forget the money, you have forgotten the KISS principle. You lent money you couldn't afford to lose. You may need to sit down with your kids and work out a future repayment schedule. Perhaps you could help them obtain a loan from a bank. But even if you can afford to kiss the money goodbye, that still might not be the best solution. It may leave too many complications behind. Unless your children are in the throes of a serious problem—illness, for example, or unemployment—resist the temptation to 'just forget it.' Instead, enjoy being gracious (especially if you think you're not going to get the money anyway). Perhaps you can find some special occasion, such as a birthday or an anniversary, when you can make a gift of the balance owed. This reminds your kids of their fiscal responsibility but at the same time shows your generosity and gets all of you off the hook.

This is not to suggest that you make such largess a general practice, especially if you have reason to think your children are not managing their finances as well as they could and should. If you believe the time is ripe, though, it's an excellent opportunity to say that you're happy to make this gift and that you believe it is time to say *Aloha* to your banking days. From this point on, they'll have to manage on their own.

Dealing With Risky Situations

What if your children should be able to manage on their incomes but don't and turn to you for loans? If they are already paying out a third or more of their discretionary income—what's left over after paying for housing, food, clothes, and other basics—they may not be able to get a bank loan, even with you as a guarantor. If so, you and they know that you have to deal with their finances.

Dealing with it doesn't mean you automatically become the banker. This may not be the best course of action for them or for you. Except in genuine emergencies, they have to deal with it themselves and accept that some changes need to be made. The best place to start is with an analysis of their finances to answer the question *where in the world does all the money go?* and to identify how they got into this situation in the first place.

If you expect that they're not going to be happy sitting down with you and doing this very revealing analysis, if you think they'll view the prospect with fear and loathing...you are probably right!

One way to handle this delicate situation is to follow the advice Machiavelli gave to his Prince: let someone else bear the brunt of giving the unpopular opinion. If your finances allow for it, offer to pay for a personal financial adviser who can help them dig out of their financial ditch. If they accept your offer but "don't have the time" to find a planner, get referrals from reliable sources, such as colleagues, accountants, or bankers.

There are different types of planners. My first choice would be a planner who works on a fee-only basis and therefore won't be pushing products that give him/her a commission. In addition to advice on how to solve some immediate problems, a good planner can offer long-range money management, including investments, insurance, savings, budgeting, planning, etc. These services don't come cheap—plan to pay about eighty dollars per hour, depending on where you live. Some planners charge a flat fee after an initial consultation during which they get an idea of the work to be done. Many people prefer an arrangement like this. Some provide free initial consultations, since the relationship is going to very personal and the chemistry should be just right. Paying for a financial planner may not be cheap, but it may be much less expensive than being stuck with a bad debt and bad feelings.

For information and a list of fee-only planners near you, write or phone the National Association of Personal Financial Advisers (1130 West Lake Cook Rd., Ste. 150, Buffalo Grove, IL 60089; 800-366-2732). If you call, a planner will call you back. If you should choose a planner who charges fees and commissions, get an up-front statement about the source of the commissions.

Alternatively, you can suggest that they look into modestly priced or even free financial counseling services offered by community agencies. These groups can give good advice on how to get out of existing debt and work with the creditors. They are usually not in a position, however, to draw up long-range plans. These services can usually be found listed in the *Human Services* section of local telephone directories or through the National Foundation for Consumer Credit (8701 Georgia Avenue, Ste. 507, Silver Spring, MD 20901; 301-589-5600). (Review the related discussion in Chapter VIII for additional suggestions.)

Bankrolling a Business

All the safeguards that apply to personal loans apply even more to business loans to your children. If you can't afford to lose the money, you can't afford to risk it. Still, a loan for a business can be easier than a loan for personal reasons. You're free to ask detailed questions about the proposed business. *What's the product or service? What are the supply sources? Is there a market? How will the product or service be sold or promoted?* You're freer to discuss how the money will be repaid, since there is the possibility that it can be repaid from the profits of the business.

If you're in business yourself or have knowledgeable sources of your own, you'll know how to evaluate the proposed venture. Otherwise, if you don't know how to judge its viability—and you're probably more interested in that than in the loan repayment—there are other sources that can help your children get started on the right foot. These same sources can sometimes lend money, which is preferable to having you as the banker.

Many universities with economics and business departments have divisions or small business development centers specifically set up to give this kind of advice and help. If the business seems viable some will help with the initial plan and stay with the business to help it develop, possibly suggesting other sources for loans as well. There are also venture capital groups and 'incubator' groups which can give advice and possibly provide capital for start-ups which meet their very stringent standards.

Other sources of low-cost business counseling are local and regional Chambers of Commerce. The Small Business Administration (SBA) offers advice and may also have loans available for qualified borrowers. The SBA-administered Service Corps of Retired Executives (SCORE) has volunteers who will counsel small businesses. Meanwhile, government agencies and foundations offer all sorts of loans and advice to women and minority groups.

This is outside help with a professional commitment. These resources can help you and your son or daughter make the right decision about starting or financing a business. Your child needs to take the initiative by seeking the best advice and resources from outside sources like these. If they can't work out a business plan that seems feasible to an outsider, why should it be feasible for you? It's not unreasonable for you to raise this question. Of course, there's always the possibility that outsiders, who must be conservative, are wrong. But at least you and your children will go into the venture with your homework done and an in-depth understanding of the risks you face.

The difference is that outside help involves only professional commitments. A parental commitment can have personal and psychological implications, especially when a loan is involved. If you deny the request, your children may feel that you are depriving them of their dream—and this may create a rift that will take a long time to heal. At the same time, if you help them, their siblings may resent the demand on your resources and the risk you're taking on.

On the other hand, you can help them reach for their dream. If they fail, they can try again or try out some other line of work. But at least you've helped give them a chance.

Only we parents can make the difficult decisions about how we should proceed. Perhaps we should be grateful that it is we who can help and not we who need the help. And if we see that our children and grandchildren have a better life because we have helped them—whatever form that help may take—then we have given a real gift to ourselves as well.

CHAPTER XVI

The Parent-Child Communication Highway

We live in the age of communication. We can talk to our children from half-way across the world, the continent, or the town. But this doesn't mean that communication between us is any easier than it was for earlier generations.

We have witnessed mind-boggling and culture-shaking changes during the past few decades. Perhaps life was easier when there were more precise and traditional demarcations between the various stages in our lives, more guidelines for behavior, and more standards to abide by. We come from and, in turn, have smaller families, so we have smaller extended families to call on. We may be increasingly mobile, but we have weaker friendship links and fewer long-time neighbors as a result.

Meanwhile, most of us enjoy levels of health and financial independence unknown to earlier generations. Many of us live alone as widows, widowers, or divorcees. More of our children are divorcees, single parents, or never-marrieds. While we have attenuated the social and cultural connections between our kith and kin, the ties that remain among our families have become increasingly important as some of the remaining fixtures of our increasingly impersonal world.

What underlies our intragenerational links is something very ancient and very eternal—something family relation-

ship specialists call "social support." Families watch out for
each other, socialize together, step in to help if needed. We
cherish all these familial "duties" as proof of family acceptance—something we sought from our parents and our
children seek from us. And we want to give it—because
without that acceptance our relationships are going to be
superficial and strained—and communication will be difficult.

Viva La Difference?

This is not to say that it will always be easy, especially when
the younger generation's values and lifestyles can be so
different from ours. Devoutly religious parents who con-
demn premarital sex may have trouble accepting their children's choices to cohabit without getting married. Thrifty
parents who always skimped to provide for the future may
not understand how their children can have big salaries and
tiny bank accounts. Seniors who always lived with gleaming
floors and polished brass have difficulty accepting that their
children and grandchildren can thrive in a house with
wall-to-wall toys, newspapers, dogs, comic books, odd shoes,
and yesterday's socks.

These differences matter. They matter a great deal, in fact,
when we can't discuss them easily or when they result in
misunderstandings, uneasy silences or, worst of all, arguments
or estrangements. Yet, we still want to know what's going on
in our children's lives, to cheer when all goes well and to be
supportive when it doesn't. And we want the same from
them. To achieve this, we have to be able to communicate.

We recognize that children have to break their attachments to us, that we have to let them go, and that this doesn't
happen in a straight line. Instead it looks more like a
cardiogram, with alternating level lines and peaks. They stay
with us, break away, come back, and break away again until
they finally achieve their own identities. Then we move on
to the next phase—communicating with our children as the
adults they have become.

Intrafamily communication that leads to and maintains truly satisfying family relationships does not just happen (even if we don't have to overcome past problems and deal with present difficulties). And we certainly cannot simply make it happen. Successful intrafamily communication will depend at least in part on our children's participation.

Typically, we have the easiest relationships with the children who have achieved their own independence. Like self-confident people everywhere, they don't need outside approval to feel secure or to move through their lives. They have well-established ideas of what's important and valuable to them and how they should live to achieve their personal and career goals. Their self-esteem comes from within. They may or may not differ with us about values, but that doesn't interfere with their love for us, their respect for our strong points, and their tolerance of our human foibles and whatever they may consider our weaknesses.

Next come the middle-ground children. We stay in touch with each other, and, despite minor and occasionally not-so-minor clashes, we get along. It may not be as easy to talk with them or to express our feelings and concerns. They may be less likely to understand us as people, not just parents, and to be critical of our shortcomings. Nevertheless, we all work at maintaining our ties, and when things don't go well, we find ways to settle our differences.

The children with whom we may have the most difficulty are those who are insecure, haven't found their niches in the world, or are unhappy with themselves and their lives. They may have problems with jobs, or friends, or marriages, but there may also be underlying and continuing parent-child issues that haven't been settled.

These difficulties can result in barriers between us, barriers which we fear may become insurmountable. It is not that there is no relationship at all, but there's no real communication. Instead it's surface politeness and superficial exchanges in routine conversation. *I'm fine...How are you?...What's new?...Not much.* We communicate almost as if we felt that they were not interested in our lives and that they didn't believe we would understand or approve what they could tell us about their lives.

How Families Communicate

Family communication is more complicated than ordinary communication. According to Professors Barbara L. Fisher, Paul R. Giblin, and Margaret H. Hoopes, it consists of two parts: *cohesion*, the emotional bonding of family members that fosters mutual support, loyalty, reliability, caretaking, the enjoyment of each other's company, and dependencies that vary as family members age; and *adaptability*, the family's ability to change rules, roles, and systems of interacting. Further, adaptability depends on the family's patterns of flexibility, leadership, assertiveness, negotiation, and giving, receiving, and using feedback.

Linguistics professor Deborah Tannen adds that communication is an on-going give-and-take. She defines it as "a continuing balancing act, juggling the conflicting needs for intimacy and independence. To survive in the world we have to act in concert with others, but to survive as ourselves, rather than simply as cogs in a wheel, we have to act alone."

Communication within a family is far more than what some authorities might define as the art of interpersonal rapport. Perhaps that definition could stand a little of the engineer's metaphor: the technology of sending and receiving messages. When there is good, in-depth rapport among us we understand the messages; we're interested, responsible, supportive, all by choice, because we love each other. We don't do this at every moment or in every instance; indeed, we often seem to be big pains to those who love us. But it's one dimension that we try to make constant in our relationships.

Communication Roadblocks

Communicating is easier said than done. In the real world, there are a number of barriers to it, and these are often amplified in the context of family. One important impediment to communication is fear. Many parents hesitate to speak their minds or give their opinions, out of fear—fear that they don't understand today's standards and viewpoints, fear that they'll offend or alienate their children, or fear that they'll be criticized for interfering. (Some parents have complained that what was once *Children should be seen and not heard* is now *Parents should be seen and not heard*.)

At the same time, children fear they'll hear a parental message they've heard many times before and don't want to hear again. They've made their own choices, but they fear they'll offend their parents or seem disrespectful if they don't agree with them on major issues. So either they sugar-coat what's really on their minds or they remain silent altogether.

If there's bad news to report—the loss of a job, a troubled marriage, a serious illness—both parent and child fear the other won't be able to handle it and therefore hesitate to reveal it. In most cases, both parents and children are mistaken. The news comes out anyway, but in a way that makes it more rather than less difficult to deal with.

There is no quarreling with these motives, but there is a quarrel with the results. Communication which is delayed, confused, or cut off is defective communication, because it leaves parents and children ignorant about what is really happening. At best, this only postpones the inevitable discovery of the truth or the permanent living of a lie. Now that we're living longer, we're looking at relationships that could span fifty years—and that is a long time to be misinformed or to feel deceived!

Getting Started

It would be so easy if we could simply transport ourselves and our children back in time to the origin of our misunderstandings. We could hover above ourselves, watch and listen to what we're saying and doing, and intervene at just the right time. We could give ourselves a chance to do it right the second time around.

Would that our communication problems were so easy to solve! More often than not, we want to communicate, but find it difficult and frustrating when we believe we have not succeeded despite our efforts. We often don't even know where to start, or even worse, we start expecting from past experiences that we are going to fail.

A major barrier to communicating is that each of us unconsciously evaluates and judges what the other person says from the perspective of our own personal and private reference points. Sometimes we are able remain neutral, but much more often we approve or disapprove and respond accordingly. The other person gets our message of approval or disapproval, even when we bend over backwards not to express it in words.

This tendency to judge is common in almost all discussion. It is intensified in situations where our feelings are involved, which is certainly the case in discussions with our children. And, the more intensely the emotions are aroused, the more likely that there will be no meeting ground, or mutuality, in the discussion. Instead, we have different ideas, feelings, judgments of what's been said, and we end up talking past each other instead of meeting on common ground.

Knocking Down the Barriers

It is possible to prevent this impasse. To have a meeting of the minds is seemingly simple: real communication happens and inflexible judgments are avoided when we listen with understanding. That means putting yourself in the other's shoes, hearing the ideas and attitudes expressed from their point of view, sensing how the situation feels to them, accepting their frame of reference about whatever you're discussing or whatever is troubling you. This is empathetic communication—understanding and not simply interpreting.

If you can listen to what your children are saying or telling you, understand how things seem to them, sense the emotional 'flavor' of what's happening—in short, if you can listen empathetically—you can release the potent forces of change (in them and probably in yourself) that become trapped beneath misunderstanding.

Carl R. Rogers, a distinguished psychotherapist, suggests this experiment to "test the quality of your understanding." The next time you have a disagreement with your children, stop for a moment and lay down this rule before continuing. "Each person can speak for himself only after he has first restated the ideas and feeling of the previous speaker accurately and to that speaker's satisfaction."

In order to keep the conversation going, you have to 'step into their shoes,' their frame of reference, understanding their thoughts and feelings so well, so empathetically, that you can summarize them correctly. It may take some practice to do effectively, but once you see their viewpoint you will almost be forced to revise your point of view, your reactions, and your responses. Much of the emotion and tension will begin to go out of your discussion, the gap between you will narrow, and the differences that remain will be reduced.

What does it take to put this seemingly simple experiment into practice? Courage, for one. You are entering someone else's world, a world you once thought you understood and now find out that you don't. It could be surprising, even upsetting. You may have to discard some of your ideas and make some changes, and change is always uncomfortable. It's human to resist and to cling to our old, comfortable, and non-threatening ways.

One benefit from Roger's approach is that it involves a commitment from everyone. You may start it unilaterally, but it is not, and cannot be, a one-sided process. When you explain what you're doing, your children, too, must be willing to step into your shoes, empathize with your viewpoint, and make changes of their own. This will be no easier for them than it will be for you. It's most difficult when the relationship between you is very emotional—but that's the very time when better communication is most needed.

If things are rocky right now, don't expect them to turn to sweetness and light right away. But there will be improvement—how fast or how gradual will depend on the issue, the depth of the conflict, and the temperaments of the people involved. There's always some accomplishment, though, even if it is a better understanding of the other person's viewpoint. That's a basis for building a mutually satisfactory resolution, one which starts when everyone lowers their defenses and opens their minds just a little. That enhances the prospect of finding some grounds for agreement. And even if a solution cannot be found, perhaps a way can be found to put the problem on hold amicably.

Communication is always fraught with challenges. Within the context of a family, it can be made all the more challenging by years of judgments and distortions. But family communication is all the more important because it is so much a part of family life and family feelings. The more we can do to make communication with our children flow smoothly, the more rewarding our ongoing family relations will become. It is certainly worth any effort we put into it.

CHAPTER XVII

New Connections On The Family Internet

Is it the devil who tempts us to offer advice to our children when they run into life's potholes? There are many times when we think we know what's best for them. (Sometimes we are even right.) For some strange reason, though, our children, like the other people we give advice to, don't always appreciate our generosity. Be it devil or angel who is whispering in our ears, when we want to offer help, there are poor ways and good ways to do it.

Should You Give Advice?

In *How To Deal With Your Parents*, Lynn Osterkamp, offers advice to our adult children about dealing with us. Dr. Osterkamp says there are parents who are "solution-givers." Using kinder words, she strongly implies that these parents are a real pain. Their children are looking for someone to listen and help them think through a problem, after which they will work out their own solution. But their pain-in-the-neck parents immediately jump in and pronounce the solution.

These children feel that they're being treated as if they weren't old enough or bright enough to solve their problems. Their parents are still authority figures and the children still want to be dutiful, so they may feel pressured to listen and to consider the advice. But, they are also adults, so they may well feel pressured to resist and to point out what's wrong with the advice. The parents then feel that they have to defend their point of view. Parents and children argue, or the children simply shut up and effectively shut off communication.

The better way is to become what Dr. Osterkamp calls a "facilitator." You listen empathetically without being judgmental, and your children think out loud while they are explaining the problem. Very often they work out the solution themselves, which is a much more satisfying course. True, they haven't received the benefit of your wisdom. On the other hand, you can be proud that you've raised capable, intelligent children.

What happens if the situation is reversed, and you have a problem? Your kids, too, may want to be helpful and jump in to offer their solution. The same devil tempts them to pass on the wisdom they've acquired thus far in their lives. Or they may feel that we need to be enlightened in the ways of their modern world. After all, they may have their stereotypes of us as senior citizens. We're set in our ways, you know, and we don't understand today's world, so they have to enlighten us. Or, they may have outdated perceptions of us left over from their childhood, just as we have outdated perceptions of them from their early days.

We appreciate their good intentions, of course. But we have other reactions as well, ranging from amusement, to tolerance, to annoyance and resistance. It's our turn to say that we need someone to listen, to be a sounding board, so that we can make our decisions.

So how do you create good intergenerational communication? There's no great secret—parents and children need listen to each other with open minds and silent judgments, to be candid while treading gently and discreetly. We all have tender spots, and there are enough people in the outside world pressing on them. Within the family we don't need to touch them.

Anger: A Major Obstacle

Good communication doesn't just happen one sunny afternoon while everyone is sitting around feeling mellow. It develops slowly and needs to be worked at consciously and patiently. One of the most vexing obstacles along the way is anger.

It's tempting to let bottled-up anger, successfully repressed during most superficial contacts, to come bursting out. There is a deep-seated belief among the general public and the psychological establishment that 'blowing your stack' or 'getting it off your chest' is a good way to ease tensions. It is tempting, but not necessarily good, appropriate, or even helpful.

Carol Tavris, a social psychologist who has studied and written extensively about anger, says this just isn't true. The causes of anger, especially in a family, are complex. A single remark or incident may start an argument, but the real cause of the anger can be a mixture of old and new feelings, hurts, and misunderstandings. 'Blowing your stack' may simply heat up or inflame some or all of them. Not surprisingly, the person who receives the brunt of the anger will have a mix of emotions in response—defensiveness, hurt, and anger. This is not the way rapprochement begins.

Defusing Arguments

Rehashing the past doesn't help smooth the communication path. It may, in fact, deepen the conflict by giving long-forgotten arguments new life. The past can't be undone; it can only be understood in context, forgiven, and laid to rest. If past differences remain, there are ways to help resolve them and to establish a new basis for the parent-child relationship.

A certain amount of change will be inevitable as our children move through adulthood, and change, by its very nature, is stressful. How the change affects you will be a very individual matter, since every family and every person in it is different. No single panacea fits all situations. But there are some ingredients that make each situation easier to pass through.

Is there a problem? Start with an open and frank analysis of what's bothering you in your relationship with your child or your child's spouse. This is the time to examine your perceptions of the problem. If you and your spouse are participants here, discuss the situation if your separate perceptions are different or conflicting. You may decide to speak to your child as a couple or to express your viewpoints individually. This will help you both deal with the problem while avoiding the complications that could result from disagreements between the two of you.

Follow this with preliminary parent-child discussions, acknowledging that you find it difficult to talk about the subject but that you want to have better communication. If you or they have more than one issue to discuss, these can be included in subsequent talks between you.

Set up the ground rules—no recriminations, no *you always do this* or *you never do that* statements. If the discussion gets tight-lips-white-knuckles bitter, it's time for everyone to take a walk in separate directions and come back when knuckles and lips are normal. If the atmosphere is still tense, set another time and try again.

Realize that there may be uncomfortable moments during these discussion. You have to decide how much discomfort you can handle—and, just as importantly, how much the other people involved can handle. It may be necessary at some point to stop and say, "Let's let this go. It's not really necessary for our discussion or understanding." You may even find some issues that will never be open for discussion.

It is important to preserve and enhance everyone's self-esteem. Make a point of complimenting the many things that your children have done or are doing well, even as you voice your complaints. Trust that they will return the compliments, if not now, then later.

Parents who have followed this path successfully learn to rehearse their comments and even to make notes about what they want to say—and then to proceed cautiously. One mother said she starts with: "Now that we've agreed that we're going to try to be more honest with each other, here's a question I'd like to ask you about a possible course of action. Feel free to give me your true feelings. I have no strong feelings on this, and I'm happy to abide by whatever you would find easiest." This is a good beginning to a potentially difficult conversation, because it introduces a difficult, potentially emotion-laden question with a simple "Here's what's on my mind, and I want to know your opinion."

The Art of Receptive Listening

These situations can be eased if we use what professionals call "communication skills" and what we might call ordinary courtesy—the golden rule observed by both parents and children. The essence of communication is that it's a two-way street. Anything we ask of our children, we are obliged to ask of ourselves, and vice versa.

Sharon Hanna, a family relations specialist who teaches communications, urges people to practice "receptive listening." It starts when we listen without interrupting. (Interruptions are often caused by the desire to defend yourself—*I never said that!*—and these defensive interruptions can turn communication into argument about as quickly as anything.) Allowing someone to speak without interrupting gives the speaker the chance to say all that he wants to say when he wants to say it. It also holds down anger and speeds up the process of agreement.

Next, listen without judging or putting down. When you put down someone, even unintentionally, the typical reaction again is a defensive one. A person who expects a put-down or a negative judgment, an *I told you not to do that* or an *I told you that would happen* is going to stop expressing thoughts or opinions rather than risk the put-down.

Listen without one-upping. A child who's looking for understanding or a chance to unburden herself after a hard day wants to be the speaker, not the audience. If your children say they didn't call, write, or do as they'd promised because they were tired or too busy, spare them the one-up: "You think that's a long work week? When I was your age I used to work seven days a week, twelve hours a day. We had to wash diapers leaning over a washtub, and we had to carry groceries and you babies up and down six flights of stairs."

So what if you worked late every night and weekend and commuted two hours to and from work? So what if it was hard to get a job because you were a woman, or a minority, or a member of the 'wrong' group? It doesn't ease today's tired feet, weary eyes, or overwhelmed feelings. George Bernard Shaw said, "If parents could only realize how they bore their children." How right he was! Maybe we should take a little oath to tell them once—well, maybe just two or three times—and then spare them our further moaning.

Some Additional Listening Tips

Listening is more than keeping your ears tuned. It's tuning your body in as well. The really good listener pays attention; maintains eye contact with the speaker with friendly, not steely eyes; responds with appropriate facial expressions— surprise, amusement, sorrow; and helps the speaker to continue talking with encouraging expressions.

Poor or obstructive listeners look away, sigh, raise their eyebrows, look imploringly to heaven when they disagree with what's being said, and wiggle around in their chairs with visible impatience. We communicate in many non-verbal ways which are often much more honest than our words. There's no point in saying you're truly interested if your body language says you're not. There's no point in saying that you're listening with an open mind when your face shows your disapproval.

Moderate your opinions by using *I* statements when you express them. *It seems to me*, or *I believe*, or *in my opinion* are softer, gentler phrases that are more likely to induce non-defensive responses when you're discussing a touchy subject.

For instance, when you say, "You shouldn't shop at that store; it's too expensive," your comments are bound to bring out a defensive reaction (even if your child agrees with you). You're being critical and using judgmental terms like 'should.' It's natural for us to be defensive when we're criticized. A gentler way would be to modify your statement—"I'll bet another service station will charge a little less than the one you're using." This seems almost elementary, but it is amazing how few of us really communicate in this way. It is effective in part because you have to change your focus and stop momentarily to think about what you are going to say. That little hesitation will do wonders if you need to temper your remark.

(And just imagine how pleasing it would be for you if, instead of saying, "Dad, you eat too much meat," your daughter or son said, "In my opinion, meat is not the healthiest food. Come for dinner and let me show you what a great Italian chef I've become.")

Setting Boundaries On Both Sides

None of this means that we should walk the entire mile to meet our children where they are standing. We have the right to expect that our children will give as much acceptance to our lifestyles and opinions as we give to theirs. There are certain things our children should not ask of us. And there are certain *buts* and *ands* that we will need to accept.

Our kids should not expect us to say we approve of everything they do, especially when saying that would be a lie. But, once we've given our reasons (calmly thought out and expressed, of course!), they have a right to our acceptance, even if we do not approve. We should spare them the nagging and the indirect criticism. "You have the right to your own wrong opinions," my sons often remind me.

Our kids should not expect us to know how we bug them until they tell us. They do take a risk when they tell us, but, once they do, it's our responsibility to listen carefully, to try to understand why they feel the way they do, and not to react defensively. By now, we are all adults, with the right and responsibility to be dealt with and to deal accordingly.

And we have a right to expect certain things from our children. We are entitled to respect for our values, even if they are quite different from theirs. We may think cleanliness is next to godliness; they may think it's synonymous with snobbishness. We may think good manners are important; they may call them politically incorrect. We may treasure family rituals and religious observances; they may consider them remnants of the dark ages of both the family and history. Nevertheless, they are important to us. Our kids don't have to bless our ways, and we don't have to expect them to.

We'd like them to keep in touch now and then, but we need to recognize that it may be difficult at times. Our children are on a safari, and they've just missed the last elephant out of the jungle. They're on a white water rafting trip and their letter lands in a waterfall. Okay, we understand. But an occasional phone call is not too much to ask. So what if nothing much has happened? They are our kids and we are their parents. There is something about that relationship that is absolutely unique, something that makes us want and need occasional contact.

The Healthy Family Mix

A healthy family is hardly one in which everyone reacts in the same way and has the same attitudes about everything. Heaven forbid! That family would probably bore each other to tears. As long as the Republicans respect the Democrats, the red-meat lovers have pasta for the vegetarians, and the Beethoven aficionados try to understand what makes the latest rock band appealing, family members feel secure, trusting, and positive about their family and their place in it.

That's the winning ticket, the big payoff, and not the impossible dream.

The happy fact is that as your children get older and have children of their own, most of them will begin to understand the pleasures and pitfalls of parenting. They begin to appreciate not only what you've done, but also who you are. If you haven't experienced this already, you will. It's a nice feeling, and an especially welcome one when it happens unexpectedly, as it often does.

That is the way it happened for Louis. While his daughter Monica was growing up, she did many things that were contrary to his advice and didn't do many of the things he recommended. One day, when she was about seventeen and very independent, Louis said he was "finished telling her what to do."

"Thanks, Dad," said Monica, "You've really matured a lot."

When our maturity finally arrives, do we want thanks from our children for the long march? The time and energy we've expended? The day-to-day anxieties? The sleepless nights? Perish the thought! Still as William Butler Yeats observed, "No man has ever lived that had enough of children's gratitude."

CHAPTER XVIII

The New World Of Divorce

The cartoon shows two little girls and a little boy playing. "Let's play house," one of the little girls says to the other. "You be the daughter, I'll be the mommy, and Roddy, here, can be my ex." How well it illustrates the world we live in today. Children know how to play their roles perfectly, because they are only too familiar with the world of divorce.

As parents we, too, are familiar with the world of divorce. We've read the statistics and some of us, though far fewer than in subsequent the generation, have even been through it. We know that fifty percent of first marriages end in divorce, and an even higher percentage of second marriages end the same way, particularly, alas, when there are children involved. The culture of divorce is so well established, in fact, that Miss Manners, the grande dame of "excruciatingly correct behavior," has gently given us some of the etiquette of the divorce scene: correct divorce announcements, deciding family loyalties, dealing with your ex-spouse's new mate at your daughter's wedding.

It's one thing to learn these facts from newspapers or TV; it's quite a different experience when your daughter or your son is the statistic. How could it be that the happy couple you toasted with champagne is now staring at the bitter dregs of a marriage that seemed to start so well? And what about the innocent victims—their children, your grandchildren?

You may not know the right thing to say, to feel, to do. If you've never been divorced you haven't experienced the stages and the depth of the trauma of divorce for the people involved. And even if you have been divorced, you cannot share or lessen the emotions and dislocations that your kids are feeling.

A parent's first reaction is often guilt. "What did I do wrong? Maybe I shouldn't have gone to work full-time until they started school; maybe I should have spent weekends with my kids instead of going to the office; maybe I was too strict, too permissive." We collect all these guilty *maybes* until we begin feeling that we, their parents, should have been able to prevent this.

The guilt is understandable—it's part of being a parent. But we also need to remind ourselves of some basics: we are the creators of our children, but they are not our creations; our children have their own identities. They are adults who have made their own choices over which we had little or no control; we cannot take responsibility if these choices didn't work well, because we are not the only influences, good or bad, in their lives.

Above all, we need to remember this: showing our guilt and distress will only increase the turmoil that the separating couple is experiencing. Not only are they in trouble, but they've also made their parents unhappy. Adding guilt to their turmoil is not what's needed at this time.

Marriage Stability, U.S.A. Style

The United States has the highest rate of marital instability in the developed world. That's not surprising considering that marriage evolved in this country within our tradition of free choice and individual freedom. In contrast to Europe, where parents and families arranged or influenced marriages, American parents exercised little control over whom, or when, their children married.

Prior to the 1930s, marriage had a contractual essence that presumed love, home, and family. Men, it was assumed, would provide support for wives and children, while women would provide homemaking and child care. Sex was part of the contract—"You can't have one without the other," as Frank Sinatra and other popular singers used to remind us.

Since the 1930s, the nature of marriage has shifted. Increasingly, marriage has come to be viewed as 'companionate.' Mutual interests, companionship, and romantic love have become increasingly important components of wedded life. Marriage increasingly has become a place where men and women look for other benefits—personal and emotional satisfaction as well as (we all hope) financial stability.

At the same time, personal and economic tremors have shaken the not-so-solid earth of marriage. The birth control pill has allowed women to enjoy sex without the fear of pregnancy—gone is the need to worry about the 'sin' of having babies without a wedding ring. And, as they pursued careers and flooded into the workplace, women have found they can be providers (though still at lower salaries), so their economic dependency has become much less of a limiting factor.

University of Pennsylvania sociologist Frank Furstenberg points out that "as emotional gratification became the sine qua non, or essential element, in the institution of marriage, divorce became an indispensable element in the institution of matrimony, permitting couples to rectify poor choice." Standards have changed. Couples no longer feel obliged to stay married for the sake of the children if love dies. They can now bury the corpses of love and marriage, using divorce as the spade.

The result has been the almost total redesign of the institution of marriage as we used to know it. Sociologists foresee few if any changes in these trends. The current high levels of divorce from first, second, and even third marriages will continue, and many children can anticipate spending parts of their lives in single parent homes. Divorce, says

Professor Furstenberg, "has become an intrinsic part of the family system." This makes understanding what happens to our adult children on their way to divorce all the more important.

The Fallout From Divorce

In this 'liberated' age there is still, if not a stigma attached to it, a perception of failure associated with divorce. Go into any bookstore and ask the clerk where to find books on divorce. Chances are, the clerk will raise his eyebrows or give you a look of sympathy. You'll be tempted to say, "It's not for me, it's for my friend."

It's small wonder our children find it difficult to give us the news. Many parents have to learn from different sources that marriage ties are getting frayed, stretched to the breaking point, or torn apart. If we live nearby, we can see it happening. If we're farther away, we may have had some hints that things aren't going well. Even then, especially if we haven't been close to our children, we may be totally shocked when we get the blunt announcement: "We're getting a divorce."

Sally went to spend her holiday with her son and his wife in San Francisco. Their marriage seemed to be a happy one between two people who had much in common. Sally looked forward to the trip with pleasure. She was on very good terms with both; her daughter-in-law even called her occasionally to ask for career advice, since they worked in the same field. The visit was uneventful. Shortly after Sally came home, however, she received a phone call. They hadn't wanted to spoil her vacation so they waited until she returned home to give the news that they were separating. To this day Sally doesn't know what went wrong.

This is not an untypical situation when thousands of miles separate us from our children, a distance that not even frequent phone calls and a good rapport can overcome. Close or distant, physically or emotionally, our kids dread having to tell us the news. Divorce is an admission of failure—a deep, painful failure. So painful, in fact, that next to death it is considered the most traumatic event in anyone's lifetime.

It's difficult, painful, and confusing for us, too, from the moment we first have to respond to the news. There is no pain-free thing to say. Even to say "I'm sorry to hear that" has an implicit criticism—they've done something that causes us sorrow. To say something bland, such as "I wish you well," may temporarily fill the space between you, but not the void.

Rabbi Maurice Novoseller has many years of experience dealing with troubled families. His synagogue, located in a suburban area dominated by couples, sponsors weekly social get-togethers for older divorced singles.

Rabbi Novoseller says that divorce is a "kind of a death," except that death can be easier to handle because it is irrevocable. By contrast, the decision to divorce is just the beginning of a process. He recommends parents follow what, in the Judaic tradition, is considered proper conduct during the traditional mourning period following a death. Say nothing, wait, and follow the lead of the mourners. When they begin to talk, listen attentively. When you hear what's in their hearts and on their minds, respond appropriately.

When your child tells you the news, your natural inclination may be to offer help. Deciding how or what to offer is difficult. You want to say, "I'm always here if you need me." But even as you say this, if you do, there's the unspoken message—you're OK and they're not. On the other hand, if you don't offer help, you may be accused later of not showing compassion. As Rabbi Novoseller says, "Parents have an interesting line to walk, but it's a no-win situation."

Speak No Evil

Never stray from this line, however, by criticizing the divorced spouse. The reasons are simple. The spouse was chosen in better days. When you attack the spouse, you are implicitly attacking your son's or daughter's previous judgment. Whether your criticism is implied or inferred, it is not constructive, especially since your child may be reproaching himself or herself on the same basis. This is especially true if you opposed the marriage in the first place; then, keeping "I told you so" out of the conversation can seem an almost unendurable restraint.

Besides, the couple may re-unite. If you intensely disliked the spouse, it's tempting to voice your opinion in no uncertain terms. But what happens if they reconcile, whether briefly or permanently? It does happen. Your child may remember what you said—never mind that he or she said the same and worse—and now resent it. Or, your child may repeat what you said to the spouse. More than one reunited spouse has been known to say, "If that's what they said, I never want to see them again, and I don't want the children to see them either." You might have to join that unhappy group of grandparents who have had to sue to see their grandchildren.

Finally, though the person may cease being your son- or daughter-in-law, he or she will always the parent of your grandchildren. Your feelings about your ex-in-law may be right on the money, but you will never be objective. You are not doing your grandchildren any favors by exposing them to the venom you may hold for one of their parents.

Accepting The News

Some parents find it hard to accept the news. Their reactions can make this very upsetting time even more upsetting. This is what happened when Harriet told her parents she was getting a divorce. It took them by surprise. Harriet's brother had been unhappily married and her sister had been divorced twice. But Harriet had never given them cause for worry. She seemed to be happily married with three children aged seventeen, fifteen, and twelve. Then she told her parents she was getting a divorce.

They were shocked, disapproving, and wanted to know why. Even when she told them, they were never able to accept her answers, choosing instead to make their daughter wrong. When Harriet explained that they were fighting all the time her mother replied, "If fighting means you don't get along and should get a divorce, I would have divorced your father long ago." When they said, "Come live with us," Harriet felt they were treating like a child. It would have been easier financially to accept their offer, but it was demeaning to her and impractical for her children, who would have had to change schools and leave their friends. Harriet had little trouble in answering, "No, thank you!"

Harriet chose instead to go it alone. She held on to her daytime secretarial job, earned extra money by doing secretarial work at home at night, and got a small amount of financial support from her ex-husband. She kept her house, her children kept their school and friends, and they all had time to get their lives together.

Throughout her struggle, what she wanted from her parents, above all—and she emphasized this passionately—was their approval. Just once, she wanted to hear them say, "Good for you, you've pulled yourself together, you're doing well." They never did.

Harriet's may seem like an extreme case, but it illustrates what sometimes happens when people get divorced. For a variety of reasons, families and friends don't always offer the kind of support that's needed. One important reason is that they don't always know what's happening and can't fathom why the soon-to-be divorcing couple act in ways that are often uncharacteristic, unreasonable, neglectful of their children, and, self-defeating. What they observe is the unusual behavior of people in crisis without recognizing what is going on beneath the public surface.

What Divorce Feels Like

To be really helpful, parents and friends need to know what happens and what it feels like to be getting a divorce.

Stress and symptoms of stress—changes in weight, upset stomach, headaches, nervousness, and general weakness—may appear well before people actually separate. They may wallow in self-pity, refuse to let go of the old relationship, or establish a new relationship with someone just like the spouse they are breaking up with—even though it was a relationship that didn't work the first time around.

The approach of divorce often produces separation shock with a mixture of disturbing reactions: denial that the relationship has ended even if the marriage hasn't; a retreat, possibly to a fantasy life where the best of the past can be found again; hostility, anger, even rage, toward the partner for the feelings of abandonment and unhappiness; feelings of guilt, kept within or projected, about what the person did that could have been done differently or didn't do and now regrets.

Sometimes separation brings much-needed relief from the extreme stress. At other times, it can produce impulsive, unproductive behavior. The separation may bring a sense of reprieve, a falling in love at first sight, a euphoria after feeling bad for so long. Some therapists call this the search for a romantic solution. But the romance is short-lived, and often people feel worse than before. It's part of the painful transition period many divorced people have before they can establish a new life.

Your separated children are experiencing pain, pain which can be so excruciating that they may even call the separation off just to bring relief. After hearing them protest that "we are absolutely irreconcilable," you then hear them tell you that they're getting back together. After the separation, the new 'free world' may be so lonely that one or both individuals may fantasize that they made a mistake separating, that they are wiser, and that they should try it again.

You, their parents, are bewildered, and so are their friends. They don't know what to believe, how to offer solace, or which one to ask to dinner. Friends may choose sides. Some friendships wither on the formerly lush vine of a couple's social set—perhaps the wife or husband was interesting only as part of a couple and not as a single. Some friends run away as if the divorce were contagious and a threat to their own marriages. People tell stories of friends not returning phone calls, rushing by on the street, or dashing into a store at the mall to avoid contact.

If this happens to your children, you can help if you mention that it is a typical reaction. This is the time when they will find out who their true, understanding friends really are. They have no alternative but to accept it, let some former friends go, and put some effort into finding new friends. In fact, finding new friends is part of the healing process, though it's not easy, and the longer the marriage the more difficult it is to do.

In *Crazy Times,* which describes her own divorce, Abigail Trafford says that the words *crazy times* really do sum up the experience. "It starts when you separate and usually lasts about two years. It's a time when your emotions take on a life of their own and you swing back and forth between wild euphoria and violent anger, ambivalence and deep depression, extreme timidity and rash actions. You are not yourself."

Sons And Daughters And Divorce

Both men and women have the same feelings of failure, rejection, abandonment, remorse, insecurity and fear. In his excellent book, *Creative Divorce*, Mel Krantzler, the founder of a divorce counseling service, says, "It matters little in the long run, whether the divorce was a mutual decision or if one partner walked out on the other. In almost all cases, the pain of emotional disentanglement affects each spouse equally, although each may feel the pain in different ways."

Men and women do experience divorce differently. It is usually the mother who stays in the home and keeps the children. Her job is often so demanding that the words *single mother* have become synonymous with a just-scraping-by standard of living, a seven-day work week, and stress. We're not yet at the point where mothers will tell their daughters to "eat your broccoli or you'll grow up to be a single mother." But her lifestyle is enough to make her single friends fearful of marriage or of having children if they do marry.

The newly single mother often has a huge daily burden, balancing child care with the upkeep of the house and the need to 'get a life.' If she's been at home with the children, she'll have trouble re-establishing her career. The stress of job-hunting, which is always difficult, adds to the stress of the divorce. Even if she's been working, she's typically earned less than her husband. This disparity in incomes sometimes means that her husband can afford a better lawyer who can pressure her into an unfair divorce settlement. Even if she prevails in court, fewer than twenty percent of divorced mothers actually collect the child support they've been awarded. Many simply give up trying to collect because going back to court again and again means too many days away from their jobs.

Getting a life? Even in the age of feminism it is still harder for women to date and there are fewer men available. Men often choose to date over a whole range of ages, but women traditionally prefer to date men close to their own ages. And just to tell a man that she has a child at home is enough to make many of them silently remind themselves not to call her again.

Men have difficulties, too, but what happens to them is frequently overlooked. After separating, they typically move to a small furnished apartment, often to one furnished with castoffs that would otherwise have been left curbside for trash collection. Their friendships with other men are often re-volve around their work, leisure, or sports activities, and these friends too often don't know how to be emotionally sup-portive.

Women are not afraid to reveal their feelings and usually have some friends who offer sympathetic ears. Men rarely have a sympathetic audience, and in this society they are still expected to hide their feelings. It's not easy to date. Ads in the personals column may produce plenty of dates, but even that is a strain. One man described it as "like being in a permanent audition."

There is a myth that men love being 'swinging bachelors' again. Some do 'score' with women to prove they're still attractive and 'first quality,' not 'seconds' or 'rejects.' But in their hearts they don't believe it. They don't join groups that might help them overcome loneliness; they rarely seek therapy, though they may need it.

They are beset by loneliness and miss their children deeply. Their status as weekend fathers can keep them from developing a relationship with their children that enhances their pride as a father. As time goes by, they are apt to feel more and more as if they're unimportant in their children's lives.

As for the children, they are the real innocent victims. Their parents, beset by multiple decisions and problems, neglect the effect of the divorce on their offspring. Yet these effects can be devastating and last a lifetime.

As parents and grandparents, we can help get everyone through these turbulent times with minimum damage. There are families who come through, if not unscathed, then with minimum damage, because they have handled the process intelligently. This is what we'd like for our children—and we can help.

We can start by realizing that they'll have to live through the mourning period and the conflicting emotions which are a consequence of the divorce. We hope that it will contribute to their growth as independent people and that they will come out of it stronger. They need to get to the point where they ask not *Who did it?* but *What went wrong, and what can be done now to have a new and happy life?*

Our actions and attitudes can help them get to that point. In the next chapter we'll take a look at some of the things we should do...and some we shouldn't.

CHAPTER XIX

Helping Your Child Through A Divorce

"I called my father," said Chris, a member of Parents Without Partners. "He's a jerk—divorced my mother when I was twelve. I told him I was getting a divorce."

"'What are you doing that for? She's a good woman,' he said. Then he hung up."

"He didn't call back and I didn't call back. I never spoke to him again."

"Who did we want to marry us? Some clerk? A strange lawyer? We didn't want that," said Charles. "We were on excellent terms with my ex-wife, and since she had recently become a judge we thought, why not? So we went to her oYce on a lunch hour, and she married us."

Here were two very different outcomes of divorce.

Chris harbored anger and resentment from his childhood, and he never let it go. It spoiled his youth and had a bad effect on his marriage. The phone call to his father had a subliminal purpose—to remind him that he had failed as a father. Chris got his revenge. His father got the bitter message. This was a classic, hostile divorce and aftermath: a bitter and enduring antipathy, a troubled child from troubled parents who never understood their son's pain, and an unhealed wound.

Charles' non-hostile divorce, by contrast, was a civilized parting. He and his first wife had married when they were twenty-somethings. They were almost thirty-somethings when their aims and career paths diverged and they realized they'd outgrown each other. Fortunately, they had no children, no need for support, and minimal antipathy. His parents, he said, "gave us very little static"; her parents still love him "dearly and deeply." As such things go, this was a good divorce.

The Good Divorce

A good divorce? That only sounds like a contradictory statement. A painless divorce, a guilt-free divorce, may be impossible, even if there are no children involved. But, according to divorce mediator and attorney Sam Margulies, a good divorce is indeed possible. According to Margulies, there are three criteria for a good divorce.

> ✧ *Legal:* The marriage is ended within a reasonable pe-
> riod of time after the decision to divorce, without
> huge legal fees that drain the family's finances and with
> a minimum of acrimony and fighting
> ✧ *Economic:* The couple is separated into two distinct eco-
> nomic units so that assets and income are fairly distrib-
> uted and the economic sacrifice is shared equally.
> Everyone in the family begins anew with about the
> same standard of living.
> ✧ *Emotional:* After the mourning period both partners are
> capable of cooperating as parents, behaving decently
> and respectfully toward each other, and going on to
> new relationships without destructive baggage from the
> previous marriage.

And one more element is crucial: the divorcing parents must give top priority to the emotional comfort of their children. This is the key, not only to helping their children through the transition, but also to facilitating their parents' own adjustment. It makes post-divorce life and future step-parenting easier and more likely to be successful.

Where do we, the parents of the divorcing couple, fit in? By staying out of the battle, according to Cheryl Vander Waal, executive director of the Center for the Family in Transition, a California-based agency that counsels more divorcing families than any other institution. It's an opinion divorce experts, therapists, and social workers emphatically endorse—for excellent reasons.

Consider the old phrase *for the sake of the children.* The divorcing couple, as we have seen, are already under severe emotional and psychological stress. They're beset by practical problems: the division of property, finding places to live, changing insurance policies and health plans, hiring lawyers, etc. They may be hard pressed to look out for the needs of their children, those innocent bystanders in the marital war.

If you get involved in their divorce, you can't be the refuge that these children, toddlers and teenagers alike, crave. If you stay clear of the battlefield for the sake of the children, you can provide the stability and the solace they need. More than that, if you can keep your cool, you can be a an island of rational thought while the divorcing couple flounder in a sea of confusion.

Staying out of the battle does not mean withdrawing because you're afraid of saying or doing the wrong thing. Nor does it mean you should stay on the sidelines and do nothing to help. This is a time when your children and your grandchildren need all the support you can give them. And there are positive messages you can give, things you can do to help the divorcing couple suffer the least upset and get on with their lives.

As parents you can encourage the couple to make their many decisions and choose their options responsibly and to settle affairs as quickly and amicably as possible. Most people, according to Dr. Margulies, even those in great emotional pain, are capable of making such responsible choices when the necessary information is presented so that they hear it.

But they really have to hear it. Remember how your children heard when they were growing up? They could hear the honk of a friend's car horn from three blocks away while a heavy-metal rock band was playing at top volume. But for some strange reason they didn't hear when you reminded them to tie their shoelaces or hurry up or clean their room. Our voices didn't resonate against that inner ear that recognizes when something is important and shouts "Pay attention!"

Our kids may still be listening in the same way. To help them, we need to reach that inner ear.

What Parents Should Know

Anger, even raging anger, and resentment are parts of a divorce—even for the person who initiated the proceedings. It may be true that "time heals all wounds," but the wounds of divorce can be particularly deep. You can be extremely helpful to your children and your grandchildren if you encourage them nonjudgmentally to find ways to control and ultimately to overcome this anger.

For some, the anger of divorce lasts and intensifies over time, with unfortunate effects for everyone, adults and children alike. The desire for revenge or a continuing need to feel like a victim sometimes leads people to use their children as weapons against the former spouse or as scapegoats for the divorce itself. As psychologists Judith Wallerstein and Carol Tavris point out, "There is a moral as well as psychological reason for managing anger after divorce and for eventually resolving it: protecting one's children as well as oneself."

Managing this anger and resentment is difficult because people suffer when attachments are broken, even when they choose to do the breaking. Emotional wear and tear ravages the spirit. The accompanying physical wear and tear—sleeplessness, digestive upsets, more-than-usual fatigue, lack of concentration—weakens the body. Everything seems more difficult, more exhausting.

People handle this emotional tempest in two different ways. Some continue subconsciously to nourish the tempest by continually reviewing their grievances. They do it when they're alone, reliving the insults, the omissions, the deception. They do it when they're with family, friends, and strangers, repeating the grievances constantly to anyone who is willing, or unwilling, to listen.

You've probably met people who tell you in excruciating detail about the horrors of their divorce—*he cheated on me every weekend...she nagged me day and night about earning more money...I felt like such a failure and it wasn't fair.* You are properly sympathetic; only later do you learn that the divorce took place ten years ago. Perhaps you have friends who do this. You know the litany so well that you turn to mentally reviewing your shopping list or planning your weekend until the complaining is over.

If your child seems to be falling into this trap, remember that he or she may be suffering from the low self-esteem, guilt, and feelings of failure that so often accompany a divorce. Your child has to deal with these feelings and overcome them, and this is not an easy task. Your pep talks—*this too shall pass*—are no help at all, even though you've said them with the best of intentions.

This doesn't mean, says Cheryl Vander Waal, that you shouldn't 'resonate' with their anger. "Justified anger is understandable and can be dealt with. Continued rage is destructive." You can listen, you can sympathize with the problems separation and divorce bring. But don't get sucked into the vortex.

That is easier said than done. Harm to your children feels like harm to yourself. You may learn facts about the marriage that make you furious. More than a few parents—quiet, law-abiding citizens all—have found themselves, to their shocked surprise, fantasizing about hiring a hit man to murder their children's ex-spouses.

Recent studies show that the women who are best able to get on with their post-divorce lives are those who stop holding on to their sense of outrage or victimization, even when their ex-spouses' behavior had indeed been outrageous and victimizing. They decided that they should remember the lessons learned from the past and then put the past behind them. The focus of this research was women, but the conclusions apply equally well to men. All divorcing children are subject to the same stresses, and all would benefit from the same resolve to get on with life.

What Parents Can Do

How much influence you can have will depend on your relationship with your children. If there is distance between you—geographic, emotional, or both—you may not have as much opportunity to make a difference. Your children may never tell you what happened or why. And you may not want to ask them, especially if your instincts tell you that they would be offended; that they might answer politely (or otherwise) that it's none of your business; that you will only exacerbate a relationship that was already touchy and is getting touchier; or that they wouldn't tell you anyway.

Still, assuming you have kept a normal relationship with your children, there are things you can do. You can gently point out that holding on to the anger can be crippling and keep them from moving on. You can encourage them to acknowledge their wrong turn, shift gears, turn around, and find a better highway.

Or, you could diplomatically suggest a 'rest stop' where they can they get some truly empathetic first aid—a self-help group of divorced people. These groups are made up of people who have been through the same trauma. They can identify with the sorrows, problems, and loneliness of a divorce and suggest some strategies for coping.

One source of information about such groups is Family Service America, a national, nonprofit agency with head-quarters at 11700 West Lake Park Drive, Park Place, Milwaukee, WI 53224 and affiliates in every major city and many small cities coast-to-coast. Its information and referral line (800-221-2681) will allow you or your child to speak directly with a Public Inquiry Specialist.

Expediting The Divorce

Another way you can help your divorcing child is to assist in getting the divorce decree as expeditiously as possible. This often involves working with lawyers, one of the frequently misunderstood characters of public life. Lawyers are trained to be advocates and adversaries—their job is to win the case for their clients. Though they may have their own opinions and feelings, it is not part of their job to judge their client's guilt or innocence—that's the job of the judge and the jury.

In *Getting Divorced Without Ruining Your Life*, Sam Margulies observes that their training in advocacy teaches lawyers "to emphasize the clients' divergent interest. They do not encourage or emphasize the common or convergent interests of the couple." Yet divorcing couples have many common interests, not the least of which is their children. These common interests could provide a basis for cooperating to the benefit everyone involved. Not that cooperation is inevitable, even with the most understanding of lawyers. If it's a bitter divorce, both sides are apt to let their emotions sway their better judgment. This may be good for the lawyer's fees and reputation, but it's not necessarily good for the client. (Unfortunately they are sometimes encouraged to squabble by the divorcing couple's parents, who do take sides and enter the battle eagerly.)

Attorney Murray Richmond (who correctly predicted, incidentally, that 'no-fault' divorces would hurt women) warns against lawyers who participate in the bloodletting. When a prospective divorce client comes to him and says she wants a lawyer who will "cut her husband's balls off," he tells her, "I'm not the lawyer you want." Such a lawyer, he says, may win for the client, but at what cost? Her life, possibly her husband's life, and the lives of their children, could be ruined in the process.

A court will grant a divorce after a settlement agreement has been reached between the parties. There are several ways to arrive at this agreement. Some divorces are litigated by lawyers. These usually involve a great deal of hostility. After protracted pre-trial negotiations between the lawyers, the divorce is often settled by the lawyers in the judge's chambers just before the actual trial. Failing this, it's settled in court by the judge. This is the kind of divorce pursued by celebrities who've gone from well-publicized intense passion to even better-publicized intense hatred.

Other settlements are negotiated by the attorneys even before any divorce action has been filed in the court. These are considered 'amicable'—though the participants may think that's stretching the word a little far—since most of the details have been worked out in advance. Clients and their lawyers meet separately, then together, to resolve any disputed issues. After they have worked out the agreement and signed it, one lawyer files the case and the court grants the divorce.

In both of these methods, it's the lawyers who do much of the work. They meet and talk with their clients, define the issues, direct all the information-gathering about finances, assets, insurance, etc., and obtain any experts if they are needed. The lawyers put the information together and then negotiate the settlement.

Lawyer-involved divorces have their advantages. They work well for couples who are too angry to meet and work well together. They also work well if the lawyers are evenly skilled, have time to give their clients all the attention they need, answer questions, explain the legal issues involved, and work well together.

On the other hand, there can be problems. If the lawyers are not evenly matched, one side has an advantage. Some lawyers are too busy to give their clients the information they need quickly or satisfactorily. At other times, the lawyers don't work well together, taking more time to negotiate than they otherwise might, while the meter ticks away the whole time.

The Mediated Divorce: A Third Option

Where it is feasible, I recommend a third type of divorce, the mediated divorce. Here the divorcing couple work together, with the guidance of a hired, independent, third party, to arrive at a settlement which is acceptable to everyone. The Academy of Divorce Mediators describes it as "a mutual problem-solving process whereby couples attempt to reach agreement on all the issues raised by their decision to separate or divorce." The mediator provides the framework of the discussion, keeping it focused on substantive issues like children, support, and the division of property and making sure that all the relevant issues are discussed fully, all within a reasonable time frame.

A mediated divorce is different from a lawyer-involved divorce in several respects. Foremost is that it is the divorcing couple who do the work. The mediator is a facilitator. In theory, especially if the assets can be equally divided and there are no children, people should be able to work out their own divorces. But when earnings are unequal or the relationship is complicated by children, people who can't even discuss loading the dishwasher without arguing may have a hard time discussing how to divorce. This is where mediators are useful. They can intervene, reduce conflicts, and reconcile differences. They are neutral, favoring neither side. Many mediators were therapists before they were mediators, so they can be sensitive to the emotional side of a divorce.

Another advantage of mediation, according to Dr. Margulies, is that "when children are involved, mediation forces the parents to talk to each other and to learn new ways to talk about issues as divorced parents." Like it or not, these parents are going to have to continue communicating, and mediation helps them learn how to do it.

Mediation also performs a number of useful services. If one partner did not participate in managing the marital finances and has to learn how, for example, mediation helps them get started. When people can participate in the discussions, they find it easier to accept the final agreement. And mediation often goes more quickly with a minimum of lawyer involvement, so it can mean a considerable saving of money for everyone except the lawyers.

This is not to say that mediation is for everyone. The divorcing couple must do all the digging and assemble all the paperwork documenting their assets. They must do some of this when working with lawyers, too, just as you have to get your files together when you have your taxes prepared. But in a mediated divorce, there is much more work to do. The couple must hire all the necessary experts, such as real estate appraisers and accountants.

Each party must be capable stating and fighting for his or her viewpoint. If one person has traditionally dominated the other, the mediator may not be able to offset the difference. If the couple shares too much hostility, they may not be able to be in the same room together, let alone have a rational discussion of their differences. When this happens, agreement is usually not possible, and the mediator may have to return the divorce to the court for a judge to decide.

Lawyers are still required in mediated divorces to answer the legal questions that come up, to give advice, and to review documents. Lawyers (or the lawyer if the couple has chosen to share a lawyer) must draft the final agreement to be sure it complies with the divorce laws of the state.

Most mediators are well trained, although there are no license or academic requirements for family mediators. Typically they are lawyers, psychotherapists, or social workers. If they are members of the Academy of Divorce Mediators, they have completed an extensive training course that includes 60 hours of mediation training and 100 hours of face-to-face mediation experience in at least 10 mediation cases. Their case reports during their training have been reviewed by the Academy. They will also complete 20 hours of continuing education every 2 years. Mediators' fees will vary depending on their background, experience, and professional training.

Mediated divorces have much to recommend them if the divorcing couple is able to take responsibility for their actions during the mediation. Mediation allows people who were once furious, sometimes to the point of yelling at each other, to cool off, speak calmly, accept compromise, and come to an agreement. Afterwards they may even learn to talk again in a friendly way. Couples often leave satisfied because they have helped make the decisions rather than having them handed down by a judge.

A word of caution, though, is in order. Divorce mediation is a fairly new field—it is only about twenty years old. Make sure you or your children check the background and experience of the mediator before hiring him or her. And, always verify the fees in advance. If you believe that a mediated divorce would help your children, the Academy of Family Mediators can provide a list of qualified mediators in your area. Its address is 1500 S. Hwy. 100, Ste. 355, Golden Valley, MN 55416-1593 (612-525-8670).

The more reasonable the divorce, the less stress there will be on the couple involved and on you. The next chapter looks further into the subject of reducing stress.

CHAPTER XX

Creative Help,
Post-Divorce

The road out of divorce hell is paved with one particular good intention which is shared by the divorcing couple, grandparents, extended family, and friends: the desire to spare the children. Every child experiences divorce differently, but all share the pain. They grieve that they've lost their family. They worry about themselves and their parents. Regardless of their ages when the divorce occurs, they feel rejected, hurt, and angry, their specific reactions varying around their personalities and their places in the family.

If they're pre-schoolers, they typically fear that they'll be abandoned—they see one parent leave and worry the other parent will leave as well. Not surprisingly some don't want to allow the remaining parent out of their sight; many revert to infantile behavior, fear falling asleep, or have toilet accidents. Some blame themselves for the divorce and change from being happy and outgoing to being sad and withdrawn.

From ages five to eight they continue to worry about losing the non-custodial parent, even if they've continued to see him or her. They are apt to suffer from feelings of guilt, loyalty conflicts, and fears of loss and rejection. Some worry that another child or a new spouse or lover will take their place in the non-custodial parent's life. Boys often show an intense longing for their fathers.

From ages nine to twelve—an age when children count on their parents as anchors—they may be angry at their parents for divorcing, and especially angry at the parent who they believe caused the divorce. They may feel anxious, lonely, and powerless; they may become antisocial or have trouble getting along with classmates and friends. Their school work may decline suddenly.

Teenagers, already anxious about the changes in their bodies and their growing sexuality, become even more anxious. Many worry about what's going to happen to them, including whether they will be able to have a happy marriage of their own—a worry that, unfortunately, often continues well into adulthood.

Grandparents' Roles

If you understand these anxieties you can fulfill two of the most important roles for grandparents of divorcees. First, you can support your adult child and possibly even the ex-spouse. This enables both of them to be the psychologically and emotionally sound parents they need to be so their children know they are still important parts of their parents' lives.

Second, you can remain part of your grandchildren's lives. Children who can count on the support of extended families benefit greatly, not only during the separation and divorce but throughout their lives. They may doubt that any marriage can last, particularly since they probably have friends and schoolmates who are also children of divorce. But if you've been married a long time, you are living examples that marriages can last and that a loving relationship can endure.

Your grandchildren deserve to have this benefit. Let them know there are other adults who think they are important and whom they can count on. Reassure them that their parents are still Mom and Dad, even if they are no longer husband and wife, and that the divorce has not affected their love or care. Tell them in words and actions that their parents still love them, just as you do. And reassure them that they were not responsible for the divorce—this is an especially important message for younger children.

You will sometimes have to walk a fine line to avoid being over-intrusive or over-involved. You cannot become the actual parents of the children—even if you want to. At the same time, you cannot simply abandon your grandchildren to the hazards of fortune.

Changed Views On The Effects Of Divorce

There is a new world of divorce out there, and our laws, social attitudes, and customs haven't totally caught up with it. Child development experts used to assume, for example, that it was better for children to be in unbroken homes, even if the parents always fought. When this practice seemed to exact too heavy a toll, particularly on wives and children, divorce became the preferred option—a broken home was an improvement over never-ending quarrels, bitterness, and/or violence. No one denied that divorce hurt the children, but the experts assumed that they recovered quickly and that the scar tissues weren't very deep.

Few foresaw that, with divorce a permanent part of growing up in America, parenting would take on a new meaning. Mothers experienced the 'feminization' of poverty. Fathers took up a mixed bag of less responsibility, ambiguity, and emotional loss. Children assumed increased and burdensome responsibilities for their parents and themselves while their opportunities declined. Everyone experienced suffering and disruption.

Psychiatrists, psychologists, therapists, social workers, and courts who worked with troubled families weren't able to respond to these new realities. Their theories, methods, and skills were forged from many years of experience with two-parent families. They had much more limited knowledge about the long-term results of divorce, particularly for the children. So they've had to treat a panoply of new family problems without the benefit of a well-developed theoretical and empirical base of experience. They are doctors treating

the visible symptoms of a new sickness without fully understanding its origins.

It's Harder On Mom

If it's your daughter who is getting divorced, she's going to
need all the help she can get She's supposed to support
herself, help support the children, and be responsible for their
daily lives. These activities are stressful even in two-parent
families. She does a day's work getting the kids ready before
going to work herself; her lunch hour is devoted to errands,
her evenings to dinner, laundry, and other domestic chores.
All week long she's the family 'heavy' (*Do your homework! Eat
your vegetables! We don't have the money for that!*) while weekends with Dad can mean movies, pizzas, and new sneakers.
Men may find her attractive—until they learn she has
children at home.

The role of single fathers hasn't been defined. 'Single
father' isn't yet a part of the vocabulary of divorce. Though
their numbers are rising, they are still only about fifteen
percent of the divorced-and-living-with-children. Non-custodial fathers have daily responsibilities only when they share
joint custody or when the kids are visiting for more than a
weekend. In theory, they provide financial support, they visit,
and they participate in decisions about their children's lives.
In practice, it often doesn't work that way.

Government statistics and private researchers define *support*, *visits*, and *participation* rather loosely, to say the least. In
her article, "Relationships Between Fathers and Children
Who Live Apart: The Father's Role After Separation," based
on 1987-88 government figures, Judith Seltzer starts by saying
that "wide variation in patterns of fathers' involvement after
separation suggests an absence of clear rules about fathers'
responsibilities." The data suggest but don't offer strong
proof, she says, that if fathers do even one of the three— i.e.
pay support, visit, or confer with the mothers— they are
more likely to do the other two.

Dr. Seltzer acknowledges regretfully that these conclusions about nonresident fathers have to be taken with a grain of salt. The government's statistics are based on a debatably adequate definition of paternal involvement. Support could mean as little as a single dollar; visits could be once a year; and only about thirty-five percent actually see their children every week. Dr. Seltzer concludes that "the father role is defined as much by omission as commission."

Why do these omissions occur? Some fathers limit contact to avoid the painful fact that they've lost their children. Others limit contact because it circumvents quarrels with their ex-wives. Still others drift away because they lose touch with their children once they're not involved in the daily activities of family life. Many men remarry and establish second families. Often the first wife and first children lose out to the second family, especially if the second marriage goes well.

Caitlin O'Meara described what happened when her father left her mother and married a much younger woman. When his new wife had a baby, he doted on the child. For the new baby, it was "designer everything." But tuition for Caitlin's college education? That was "a hassle." (This is not an unusual situation, however. Many men, even those with college degrees and well-established professional careers who have consistently paid child support, stop paying when their children reach college age. They feel their responsibility has ended.)

A Case In Point

The divorce history of one family illustrates what can happen. The Smiths had a traditional marriage. Both were college graduates; Frank had gone on to get an M.D. while Barbara chose the career of wife and mother to Melanie, Sally, Peter, and Michael. They lived in an affluent suburb where Dr. Smith had a lucrative practice. When Michael started kindergarten, Barbara began to work as school teacher. She overlooked her husband's casual affairs, which were well-known in their small-town community. Then he fell in love with another woman. After many quarrels, they decided to separate. At the time Melanie was sixteen, Sally fourteen, Peter, twelve, and Michael nine.

They both knew the children should be prepared for their separation and divorce, but, like most parents, they didn't tell the kids until the very day that Frank threw his clothes in a suitcase and left. Melanie, the oldest, remembers being the least upset, because "at least I grew up with a father, something my sister and brothers didn't have." But she still felt "hurt and abandoned." Sally was furious with her father, and remains so to this day, They have little contact. Peter, always the family conciliator and defender of his father, tried very hard to "see both sides" and said, "Maybe Mom wasn't always easy to live with." Michael felt abandoned, cried all the time, and asked, "Why doesn't Daddy love me?"

It was a question their families on both sides asked as well. They were all horrified. Barbara's mother refused to speak to her ex-son-in-law for four years, saying her first "Hello" at Melanie's college graduation. Frank's mother blamed herself and felt that in some way it was "her fault" that her son could walk out on four children. She was so ashamed that she couldn't bear to talk to her grandchildren.

Barbara felt as if the bottom had fallen out of her life. She kept the house, so the children could continue at the same schools and keep the same friends. But money for clothes, recreation, vacations, and college tuition was tight. She made a life for herself, kept her job and her friends, and helped send her kids to college, no thanks to Frank. She was, and is, says Melanie, "a terrific parent."

Frank followed a different and unfortunately not too untypical pattern. He failed to keep his promises of frequent visits—sometimes six months went by—and neglected his promises about money. When Peter said he wanted to spend his junior year abroad, Frank told him, "If you will forego that I'll pay to send you to a better college." But he reneged even on that promise. Gradually, his daughter said, he lost the "emotional closeness that fathers have," even though he still "exercises some control by paying or withholding tuition." Melanie does not use the same complimentary description when referring to her father.

Fortunately, relatives on both sides "rallied around," says Melanie, though they lived several states away. They kept in close touch with phone calls, visits, even plane tickets so the families could spend holidays together. Melanie said this was important for sustaining her and the rest of her family.

Different Views Of Fathers

Studies of the divorced family show that children hold onto their favorable image of their father, even if it's partly fantasy, even if they rarely see him, and even if he doesn't deserve the favorable evaluation. Children need their fathers, whether they are toddlers or near-adults getting ready to leave home.

They can be realistic, however. They know when he's not living up to his responsibilities to love them, to be interested in their lives, to set an example, and to provide for them. But another part of them looks at him with compassion and forgiveness: maybe Mom *wasn't* always so easy to live with. Whatever his history of rejections, his failure to keep promises, and his long absences, they still hold onto their internal images of father as a loving, decent person.

And, in truth, there is another side. There are mothers who go out of their way to separate their children from their fathers. Sometimes they assign blame and mete out punishment. *If he doesn't pay support, why should I let him see the children?* (And he says, in reply, *If she won't let me see my children, why should I pay support?*) Some mothers use support money more for themselves than for their children. Sometimes they feel such animosity and desire for revenge that they use anything, including the children, as their weapons of choice. Sometimes the mother's career decision requires a long-distance move, making it difficult for the father to see his children. Whatever the reason, while the children are the immediate victims, fathers are victimized, too. One of the unexplored dimensions of divorce is the price that men pay.

Not all men pay this price. Some men do seem to have it all. They make a mistake the first time around, so they choose another mate hoping to benefit from their previous experience. Often wife number two is younger, sexier, more acquainted with his world. Their second marriages may be very successful.

But many other men can't make this choice without paying a heavy price when their ties to their children are weakened or severed. They don't have relationships with their children that allow them to help their children grow up successfully. If the mother has remarried, they feel they've been replaced by the stepfather, that their children don't need them, that they are less of a man. If their children are estranged, they must face their accusations or their indifference—and this becomes one more reason why they stop visiting.

Young men are particularly vulnerable, according to Judith Wallerstein. They "divorce their children along with their wives." In an intact marriage they would have matured by taking both responsibility for their children and pride in what they were doing. As weekend fathers, they never acquire this maturity. On the surface, they may seem to enjoy being free, flitting from woman to woman and shirking responsibility. But this is counterbalanced by having no one at home to talk to when life doesn't go well, no one to share long-range hopes and plans with, no pride in their family. Meanwhile they still have financial responsibilities, guilt if they can't pay child support, and the loss of self-esteem for their part in the failed marriage. If it's your son, he hurts—and you hurt with him.

Another Case History

Not all divorces end in desperation. Bob and Marie Jones were divorced when their daughter Paula was twelve. Though their marriage seemed strong, it was undermined by a strong current of conflict that led to frequent quarrels. One summer day, Bob took Paula aside. He was so angry, he told her, that he couldn't stay married any longer. He "didn't think you should be subjected to my anger," but he told her, "I'm going to see you very often." Then, he picked up his suitcase and left. Paula was so devastated she shut herself in her room.

During the following days, both Bob and Marie spoke with Paula. Both of them reassured her that they still loved her and that they would continue to spend time with her, even though both realized that their marriage was over. In retrospect, Paula said, these reassurances helped her adjust to the fact that there would be no reconciliation. Neither told Paula until later the real reason for the divorce—Bob realized that he was gay and wanted to live his life accordingly.

Marie had already been working part-time as an accountant; she now went to work full-time. She had financial problems, though, and wasn't able to hold on to their home, so she and Paula moved to an apartment close by. It was a difficult and confusing time for everyone, but Bob never failed to pay support. He also never failed to see his daughter. Two or three times a week he came for her and, when she was older, took her to lunch, on outings, or to visit his business friends. Paula remembers with pleasure that she went to her father for advice as well as to have fun together.

Because she was an excellent student, Paula won scholarships and student loans, but they never covered the full cost of her college tuition. When she needed $2,000 one semester, her father came through with the money in short order. Bob and Marie also stayed good friends, often going out to dinner together, and Bob remained very much a part of the family, always on hand for holidays, parties, or graduations.

Paula also became been friendly with Bob's lover. When Bob died, Paula, Marie, and Bob's lover all went to the funeral together. (Interestingly, when they viewed the body, both Marie and Bob's lover commented that something was amiss—Bob's hair had been parted on the wrong side.) Paula mourns her father, whom she remembers as a "great guy" and a positive influence on her life.

Decisions For Us

We can be part of the problem, or we can be part of the solution. We could drop out altogether. After all, our adult children made their beds—sometimes even against our advice—and unmade it as well. Now they have to live with the consequences. Some parents who've been divorced themselves feel this way. *We lived through it,* they say. *What's the big deal?* Just as everyone's marriage is different, so is everyone's pain, and the fact that someone else has suffered doesn't make anyone feel any better.

Other parents say, "We don't want our children to go through what we went through; we want to be part of the solution." But they don't always know how to do it. If the academics and family theory experts haven't yet been able to offer guidelines on what's best for divorcing couples and their families, is it any wonder that we, too, have problems in knowing the best way to proceed?

Still, proceed we must. We can be support systems, mentors, listening posts. We can set the tone for the other members of the family and even for the other grandparents. We can show them how to deal with the new realities of divorce and be the successful case histories that the academics would like to draw on. "Call us up," we can say, "we'll tell you what works."

What To Do And Not To Do

Some things work, and some things don't, according to Bev Bradburn-Stern, Director of Community Education and Training at Families First, the Atlanta-based agency for helping divorcing families. In 1988 Ms. Stern founded the *Children Cope With Divorce Seminar for Divorcing Parents,* a four-hour seminar which Georgia courts require divorcing parents to attend. The seminar, which focuses on the effects of divorce on children, helps parents understand the pain their children are feeling and suggests some ways to reduce the trauma. Ms. Bradburn-Stern has trained people all over the country to give similar courses, which have now been adopted by more than thirty states as prerequisites to a divorce.

Bradburn-Stern says that parents can help their sons or daughters define the problems. Her familiar advice: listen without interrupting, and let your children unburden themselves. Then ask them to tell you what they would find helpful. You can make life easier for your grandchildren by being a listening post for them as well. They, too, need someone to talk to; as one divorced child said, "Be an ear for the kids to tell their troubles to." You can also be a buffer, helping other relatives deal with the divorcing family.

"We got sick of people assuring us that we'd be all right," said one young woman, because to her this meant, "You're not going to be all right." Grandchildren can be hurt and annoyed by intrusive questions, such as "Have you seen your father lately?" or "What did your father have to say to you?" If you're asking this question as a way to show you're interested in them and would be happy to listen to what they want to say, this is not the way to do it—you're pressing on a sore spot. Instead, start the conversation by saying something open-ended like, "What's going on with you?" Then, if they want to, they'll tell you.

Be wary of doing things that may have an unintended potential for harm. Don't become what Bradburn-Stern calls a "smother family" by trying to take over and solve the problems, smothering your child with advice in the process.

You don't really know the intimate details of your children's lives, and you probably won't be able to find them out. You are therefore not in a position to give good advice. Besides, you couldn't solve all the problems, as much as you wish you could. You have to resist the temptation to rescue them. When you put yourselves forward as a rescuer, you're saying to your kids that they're not capable of rescuing themselves. You are encouraging dependency, which is the last thing you should be doing right now.

Money Helps

The desire to avoid encouraging dependency can conflict with your wish to help your divorced child and your grandchildren financially. It doesn't have to; there are ways to help that will make them stronger, not weaker. Still, there's no escaping the hard truth that two cannot live as cheaply as one if they live apart. One almost inevitable side effect of a divorce is a reduced standard of living for everyone.

Your goal should be to help—to pay for the fishing rod but not the fish so your children will be able to catch many fish on their own. Paying for a specific purpose is preferable to a loan. It doesn't require an immediate outlay of a large sum of money, and it doesn't carry an obligation to pay back a loan (which, as we have seen, may not always be possible). Paying nursery school bills, for example, makes it easier for your daughter to hold a job. Paying for private school tuition can offset the questions that a new public school can raise. Putting aside money for college tuition, itself a good investment in your grandchild, allows your child to pay more attention to immediate expenses. (One divorce lawyer even recommends paying for counseling for the children. He is still shocked by how people use their children as hostages or weapons during a divorce and thinks they deserve some professional help if they are to survive their parents' mistakes.)

Sam Margulies points out that one of the most important assets divorced people have is themselves. An investment in their careers—which could involve anything from taking night classes to changing jobs to changing careers—can significantly improve their chance to secure their future. If making this investment seems like a good idea, you can make a real contribution to their economic security and to their self-esteem by helping them with it.

Civility Is Important

Jennifer Weiner described her feelings as a twenty-something child of divorce. "What we need for parades," she said, "are some jumbo divorce-appropriate holiday balloons, the kind that could join the lineup of large parades. There could be a giant Dad balloon on one side of the street, a giant Mom on the other. And floating between them could be their young adult child, bouncing every which way tethered to nothing at all."

As grandparents, we can supply that tether. We don't have to live close by, have lots of money, or sacrifice ourselves to do it. Regular phone calls, planned visits during school vacations, trips to the mall together with little gifts as treats…these work just as well because they provide reassurance that there's a family of grandparents, uncles, aunts, and cousins who care about the kids.

And there is one more essential ingredient we can supply: civility. Even if you think your ex-son-in-law is an unalloyed bastard or your ex-daughter-in-law is a manipulative bitch, they are still parents to your grandchildren. One of the most vital elements in the well-being of children is the belief that they have parents who love them and will take care of them. If you challenge this belief with your actions, you undermine your grandchild's sense of well-being.

Unhappily, your own daughter or son may be doing this very thing. If you have any influence, by all means discourage this. In the long run, curbing the anger will be in their own best interest, because the less-troubled the child, the easier the adjustment, not only to the divorce, but also to the future. And if your efforts to encourage the two parents to be civil are not successful, at least your grandchildren will know they can turn to you if they need to stand in neutral territory.

Keeping Your Life In Balance

Especially in the beginning, there may be times when your children and grandchildren need you, and you'll give as generously as you can of your time and your help. But you can't, and shouldn't, make their troubles your troubles. You have your own needs and goals, and there are limits to how much you can give your adult child and your grandchildren. This is particularly true financially; you must plan for your retirement, including what seem like inevitably increasing medical costs.

"You have to keep your own life in perspective," says Dr. Eric E. McCollum, a family and marriage therapist. "Sacrificing your own happiness will only build resentment." One of the best things you can do, he says, is to set limits and feel free to say *no* if you are asked to do something that is beyond those limits. Each of us will have our own limits. You need to discuss them with your spouse, then with your daughter or son, so that the limits are understood clearly and no one builds up a cache of resentment.

The Recovery Room

You will know when the recovery is on the way. The resentment and bitterness taper off despite the occasional flashes of anger. Your children spend less time complaining about problems and more time trying to solve them. They begin to call old friends and renew their networks. They work on building new lives—taking courses, entertaining, going out. They take a dispassionate view of the opposite sex, recognizing that not all women are bitches and not all men are bastards. They accept their divorce as a solution to a self-destructive marriage, not a punishment for failure. They find workable ways of meeting their responsibilities to their children and stepchildren.

For your part in this, congratulate yourself! You've helped them become whole again.

CHAPTER XXI

Fiscal Fitness: Clarity Begins At Home

Do you want to do yourself and your adult children a tremendous favor? Don't do what the following people did.

Widow *A* believed life was about teaching children, volunteering for good causes, and growing a gorgeous garden. Life was not about money—that was being too materialistic. She simply endorsed her teacher's salary checks and gave them to her husband, who managed their money skillfully and preferred that she keep out of it. Then her husband died. Though they were very well off, the bills went unpaid, her health insurance expired, she worried about paying for groceries. Finally, creditors began to send her nasty threatening letters. She called her son, who flew in from across the continent to take charge. It took him two years, many airplane trips, huge phone bills, and a few quarrels with his mother to get everything in order.

Once a month, Widow *B* gathers all her bills, bank statements, and stockbroker's reports and drives twenty-five miles to her daughter's home for help with her finances. She comes at the convenience of her daughter, who has a busy law practice and not a lot of patience. Widow *B* accepts what her daughter says and does what she says should be done. Her son-in-law considers the whole arrangement an imposition.

Widow *C* lived modestly with her husband for many years. Only after he died did she learn that they had plenty of money and that she could have had the larger apartment and more modern kitchen she'd always wanted. She is still resentful. Her daughter and son feel they were cheated of the opportunity to attend the first-rate colleges they wanted to attend instead of the local colleges they thought were all they could afford. Neither of them has especially fond remembrances of their father.

Ignorance has no sex bias. Widower *D* let his wife handle all their finances; he didn't want to take time from his work as a historian and writer. It was a shock when she died suddenly. He wasn't even sure what bank they used, let alone where the bank books were. He was much too embarrassed to confess this to his children, so he borrowed money for food and gas from two good friends. When he finally told his friends of his plight, they rescued him with an additional loan and a recommendation to an accountant, who got the widower's affairs in order—for a sizable fee.

Serious illness, accidents, long recovery periods, and other personal crises can wreak havoc on the uninformed. When spouses don't know or are too distraught to remember where vital papers are kept, when they can't or won't keep track of the payments that have to be made, when they aren't able or willing to manage routine finances, there are immediate problems. These only add unnecessarily to the stress. If adult children have to be called, their lives are disrupted to fill the breach, even though there is no reason for them to be any more knowledgeable than their mothers or fathers.

The Financial Fire Drill

Stephan R. Leimberg, a professor of taxation and estate planning at The American College, compares the situation to a fire. "Imagine your home is on fire," he says. Flames and smoke are everywhere, and in the darkness your spouse is frantically trying to get to safety. He or she makes it, because weeks before you had a fire drill. Your spouse knew where to go, what to do, how to react.

Now, he says, imagine a serious illness or accident has incapacitated you, but you haven't held that fire drill. How would your spouse cope? Would he or she barely manage after several chaotic months, manage adequately but not well after some time, or manage expertly? What would happen there were a death in the family? How much help would you need? How helpful could your children be? Will there be a good or bad ending? It's not just a question for the surviving spouse; it also affects your heirs, adult children, and grandchildren.

So, if you want to do yourselves and your adult children a really big favor, make it easy for them to get the information they need to tend to your affairs or to settle your estate.

This can be easier said than done. Sometimes the better-informed spouse may have deep-seated, subconscious reasons not to give up control and the power it brings. Sometimes one spouse has to admit that money is being spent in ways the other spouse doesn't know about and possibly wouldn't approve. Sometimes it's just that one spouse can't stand the thought of someone messing up the neat files and meticulous checkbook. And sometimes the ill-informed spouse either resists taking on the responsibility or fears it's beyond her or his ability to learn.

Whatever the problem, it can become a major headache if the ignorant person suddenly has to take charge. There are good reasons why financial responsibility should be shared. First, it's fair. Since a lifestyle is determined by spending decisions, everyone should have a voice in making these decisions. Second, it's effective. Sharing decisions gives both partners the hands-on experience that can make for better decisions and actions. Third, it improves the chance of success. Individuals who share in decisions have a stake in making them work.

On the other hand, ignorance and incomplete sharing can extract a big price in cash and in personal relationships.

Badly shared financial information can literally mean that money which could help a spouse live in a better apartment or a grandchild attend college ends up in the hands of the tax collector. Or, it could set sisters and brothers against each other at a time when they should be brought closer together.

Enter The Psyche

Psychological problems are sometimes hidden causes for resisting discussing finances. Talking about money means facing some facts of life. A husband never did get as high on the corporate ladder as he'd hoped for; a wife's design business never expanded beyond the in-home studio. Medical bills have begun to increase and will continue to do so. Unless someone wins the magazine sweepstakes, current income isn't going anywhere.

If it's the husband who handles the money—and this is still more often the case even in this liberated age when both husbands and wives are equally willing to be ignorant— wives have a very delicate role. They know that women live up to seven years longer than men. They may hate the thought of losing someone they love. They may dread the prospect, if they haven't started, of handling their finances. Or they may simply have grown tired of clenching their teeth every time their husbands reproves them for raising the subject.

It's human to want to avoid these situations, but money questions can only be avoided for so long. Ultimately they will be discussed, one way or another. It is better to make the choice to discuss them now, when decisions can be based on the best information at a relaxed time, rather than having the choice thrust upon you at a moment of stress. And if properly approached, the reluctant spouse may actually be relieved to share the burden.

Getting Down To Business

As with so many things, tact and diplomacy work wonders. Approaches like the following are non-confrontational and do not threaten anyone's autonomy or self-esteem:

✧ *We have worked so hard to accumulate our assets. We don't want them wasted or frittered away through carelessness or ignorance. If I alone were responsible for managing, I'd want to know how you would manage.*

✧ *So many things have changed since we made our decisions about our wills, or insurance, or investments. Probably we should review things to see if we should make any changes now.*

✧ *With so much divorce going the rounds, even though our children seem happily married, who knows what the future will bring? Maybe we should be sure our children will be secure, no matter what.*

Michael J. Amato, a C.P.A. and Certified Financial Planner who has successfully counseled many widows, says that too many husbands think that putting everything in writing is guidance enough. One client left his wife a twenty-five-page letter describing everything from handling their finances to changing the air-conditioning filters. But she had no practical experience and was absolutely overwhelmed by all she had to do. Fortunately for this widow, Mr. Amato was as patient as he was trustworthy. He warned her not to be rushed into making any changes until she'd taken ample time to think about what she wanted to do. Widows are often considered fair game for less scrupulous planners and well-meaning relatives and friends.

Your adult children also have to be reminded that money talk has psychological overtones, since money represents status and authority. In their desire to be helpful, they may make decisions for a parent without consultation. Many men in particular associate control over money with manhood and feel very demeaned if they don't have some control. Decisions must be made jointly, or the parent involved will be robbed of his or her autonomy and self-esteem.

It's often painful for parents who have taken pride in being strong and self-reliant to swallow their pride and ask a child for help. The difficulty is compounded if the child lives far away, making it necessary for the child to arrange for an extended visit. If time is short, the parent may hesitate to ask questions and simply accept what the child says is best—which may or may not be best thing to do.

There is no good reason why these situations should exist. If they do, the time to make changes is when you can do it leisurely without outside pressure. It not only helps you, but it also helps your children. They may have hesitated to ask important questions for fear of seeming avaricious. Letting them know that you're doing this eases their minds about the future.

Your Personal Information Checklist

One key to sharing financial management effectively is to make information available. Among the most important pieces of financial information are the following:

- ✦ *Art, antiques, and other collectibles*: Do you know how valuable your collection is? The fact that your mother told you it was valuable or that a well known artist appears to have signed the back isn't enough. You need an expert appraisal, not only for insurance, but also so you can know the market value.
- ✦ *Automobiles*: Titles, registrations, and insurance policies should be assembled where they can be easily found.
- ✦ *Bank accounts:* Keep a list of the names and addresses of the banks where you have checking and savings accounts. Include your account numbers and some indication about where you keep canceled checks and bank statements.
- ✦ *Debts:* Make sure you keep an up-to-date list of the people or institutions to whom you owe money. Include the amounts, terms, and due dates and some notation as to where relevant paperwork is filed.
- ✦ *Durable power of attorney*: In case you become incompetent, a durable power of attorney will allow the person you designate to make important decisions for you. Keep a copy of the paperwork where someone else can find it easily.
- ✦ *Employee benefits, including health and retirement plans:* Whoever handles your affairs will need to be able to claim your rightful benefits.

❖ *Insurance policies*: These include your life, health, veterans, homeowners, rental or vacation properties, accidents, disability, and other policies. Being able to find these documents makes filing claims a lot easier.

❖ *Investments*: List the numbers of the certificates of deposit, stocks, bonds, mutual funds, etc. It's a good idea to have copies of the certificates if the originals are kept at a brokerage house.

❖ *Loans:* Make a list of those people who owe you money, including names and addresses, amounts, terms, and due dates.

❖ *Personal Records.* These include Social Security and Medicare cards, birth, marriage, separation and divorce records, prenuptial agreements, military discharge papers, business or professional partnerships, etc.

❖ *Safe Deposit Box*: Make a list of the contents and note where the keys can be found.

❖ *Tax Records (federal, state and local):* Taxes are going to be paid; they're one of the two certainties of life.

❖ *Trust funds:* List any that you've granted, those for which you are a trustee, and those in which you are a beneficiary.

❖ *V.I.P. (Very Important Persons) List*: Keep an up-to-date list of your lawyer, accountant, insurance agent, banker, stock broker, doctor, business associates, and any other people with whom you have daily or essential contact.

❖ *Will*: Note the location of the original and any copies.

Once you have all this in order, make sure that others know where to find it. You'll need a filing system for keeping and maintaining this data. Both you and your spouse should understand the system and be able to use it easily. Your children should also be able to use it if the need arises. Schedule a regular review, semi-annually or annually, and update your records to keep them current. If you have made any major changes, let your adult children know about them.

Share The Burden

You will probably consult most of the records only rarely. On the other hand, some of your money management will call for your fairly frequent attention. These are areas where taking turns can be quite beneficial. Even though your household financial management tasks may have been divided according to each person's preferences, abilities, or habits, switching tasks now and then will help everyone understand the big financial picture. If one of you is the family banker who always pays the bills and balances the checkbook, turn the job over to the family spender every now and then. If one of you is the family investor who always deals with the stockbroker, let the other check on the investments and deal with the stockbroker.

Be forewarned: this could lead to family fights. If you are the family banker and keep your immaculate checkbook always balanced to the penny, you may resent seeing scratchouts and discovering that the bank statement is accurate "within a few dollars." If you are the family investor who never forgets to mail the bond-payment check in plenty of time, you may find it annoying to have to dash to the post office and send a check Express Mail.

This doesn't have to lead to problems. The immediate solution is to remember that nobody is perfect. There are lawyers who don't have wills, hot-shot brokers who drive their tax accountants crazy with sloppy records, and accountants who neglect to call their lawyers about changes in tax laws. You can aspire to perfection, but until you achieve it you can simply work at it.

The long-term answer is to remember that by dealing with present problems today you're preventing much more serious ones tomorrow.

When Janice daRosa's widower father became a victim of dementia, Janice was called on to manage his affairs. She needed some very important papers and spent many frustrating hours searching, but she couldn't find them. An attorney herself, Janice knew how to arrange for duplicates, but that would have meant inevitable delays and substantial extra fees. Fortunately, she was a lot luckier than most of us would have a right to expect. One day, when he seemed alert she said, "Listen to me, Dad, where are the ... documents?" Without a moment's hesitation he told her precisely where they were, in one of the few places she hadn't looked.

Incapacity and incompetence are only two of the fears that many of us face as we age. Even if our spouses and our children are patient, level-headed, easy-going, and dutiful to a fault, we still don't want to become dependent on them. The time to make sure we won't be is when we are well and relatively objective about our lives and affairs.

The Ultimate Responsibility

It may not happen for years or decades, but sooner or later we are all going to leave our loved ones. When that happens, your spouse and children are going to be going through an emotional, stress-laden period. Is it fair for you to burden them with the task of settling your affairs?

Calling in a financial planner, a good friend, or business partner to take over and make all the decisions in this time of grief might seem like a tempting idea. After all, it would shift the burden away from your spouse and your children. It would, however, be a serious mistake. Even in the best of all possible worlds, no one cares as much about your affairs as you do. Family members will be involved anyway, even if only because someone must find and put in order all relevant documents.

Unless there is absolutely no alternative, I recommend that you not abdicate and turn your money over to someone else. You and your heirs will be much better off if you educate yourself, use your common sense, listen to the advice you're given...then make your own decisions. You and your heirs will have to live with what you decide.

A well planned will can save everyone a lot of grief. It can be carefully crafted to take advantage of the latest tax breaks and maximize your control even after you have left this world. But a will can also be a personal expression from your heart. Stephan Leimberg, in fact, emphasizes that a will should satisfy the person who makes it. We should feel that our will provides us with one last opportunity to do what is right for our families.

This is not to say that anticipating our passage should bring joy to our hearts. And our children may not like to talk about it any more than we do. We've always been part of their lives. They have never known a time when we weren't there. It can be strange and painful for them to think that the day will come when we won't be around. They may not feel comfortable talking about our mortality. Yet talk about it we must, and this is the subject of the next chapter.

CHAPTER **XXII**

A Will And A
Weighing Of Options

Where's a family, there's a will. Where there's property, there's a will. Where there's a family and property, there are gift decisions to be made. These are rarely simple. As the Roman poet Ovid discovered two millennia ago, "to give is a thing that requires genius."

To be a genius about estate decisions would be a challenge to test Solomon. "Every family is unique, like fingerprints," says C.P.A. and Certified Financial Planner Michael J. Amato. Even the law recognizes the complexities. According to Joan Wexler, lawyer and dean of Brooklyn Law School, there are no generalities in family law, because every family is so different.

We think of wills as legal documents. They are that, but they can be much more. They are also a means, as Dean Wexler points out, of affecting behavior. They can build family harmony or set off a feud. They can affect the future. They can be used to provide security or misused to set up unwelcome controls.

Wills should come with a *Handle With Care!* label. Inheritance presumes a death, and talking about death is never easy, even in families who communicate easily. It is still more uncomfortable in families who have trouble communicating. Nevertheless, the experts who specialize in estate law—lawyers, accountants, and financial planners—agree on one thing: regardless of how well you communicate, the best way to handle the subject with care is to discuss your plans with the people who will be affected.

A family meeting to discuss your ideas can help you make the best decisions about passing on your property. The discussion can even bring a family closer together, as everyone realizes that no one is going to be around forever.

Before your meeting, however, remind yourself of one essential consideration. You take priority; you are your primary responsibility; you must provide for your own future before you concern yourself with that of your children. In fact, by providing for yourself, you will relieve them of that potential burden.

Your Will

A will serves five basic purposes. It permits the easy distribution of assets. It provides for access to funds for immediate expenses—bills, taxes, funeral expenses, etc. It guarantees, as far as possible, that your survivor's lifestyle will continue. It minimizes or eliminates taxes. And it provides for the continued management of assets, such as investments, property, or a share in a business. Both husband and wife should have wills.

A will signals an end and a beginning and provides new responsibilities for the survivors. It names an executor who will be your representative after your death. Naming someone as an executor is an honor and a sign of your trust. But it's also asking someone to take on time-consuming, worry-and-anxiety-producing responsibilities. An executor must ascertain the value of your assets, pay creditors, settle taxes due, and then distribute the assets. Even an uncomplicated will involves reams of paperwork, scores of forms, chores, errands, busywork, and legal procedures. The job can easily take a minimum of a year or more to complete for an uncomplicated estate. Having your affairs and papers makes a big difference to your executor, who quite often will be one of your children.

The business of wills, trusts, and executors—probate, for short—is the business of technicalities that must be taken care of. There are laws and procedures to be followed and lawyers and other estate-planning professionals to provide guidance. Probate is a specialization entirely its own.

Remember that wills are not written in stone. They can be changed if new conditions dictate. Don't make any changes without the advice of a lawyer, however. New wills and amendments to old ones need to be properly witnessed in order to be valid. To prevent confusion, destroy your old will.

What Do We Tell The Children?

The most difficult part of probate is often the communication. Should we tell our children how rich, or how poor we are? Why? Why not? When and where should we tell them? How much detail should they know?

Will they tell their spouses or their lovers? Probably. What effect will that have? Will the news of an inheritance mean that the no-goodnick artist your daughter is supporting will try to convince her to marry him? Will your son-in-law want a loan to start that business he's been talking about, a business you think is doomed to failure? Will your too-laid-back son or daughter blow it quickly and foolishly and end up with nothing?

If possibilities like these are on your mind, certainly discuss them with a lawyer trained in estate planning who might know ways of overcoming them.

Probate matters can make wonderful soap-opera scenarios. Just talk to an estate lawyer, particularly one with wealthy clients, and you will hear all sorts of horrendous stories about parents vs. children, children vs. parents, and children vs. children. Fortunately, these will be the exceptions. More typical is that your children are just as concerned about your future as you are about theirs. They may want you to have enough to take care of yourselves as you get older, to provide for a sister or brother who needs special attention, to provide protection for yourselves and others by writing a will. They may be hesitant to bring the subject up, however. You will relieve their anxiety if you initiate the discussion.

'Discussing' does not mean that you should list all your assets precisely, down to the last dollar in your bank account. If you don't like that idea, you're not alone. Some parents are afraid that doing this will make their children, if not lazy, perhaps less-inclined to push hard to be successful on their own. Other parents fear that revealing the specifics would permit the children to figure out how much they can ask for. Still others fear that if their children know how much money is at stake, their behavior might be motivated by money. Are they suddenly more attentive, now that they know there is money there?

Preparing For A Family Meeting

It is not necessary to spell out exact amounts. It's your business, as long as you remain independent and self-sufficient. (If you're not, the question of financing and arranging taxes for entry to a nursing home may come up. You will have to be a little more forthcoming about your assets.)

Most experts agree that the family should meet to discuss your will. But there is a great difference of opinion about the best time to meet. When asked about the optimal timing for the best outcome, some suggest a happy occasion—a wedding, a holiday celebration, a reunion. Others disagree, saying these emotional events are too distracting. Still others suggest after a recovery from a serious illness, when people are naturally tuned in to the future.

Nor do they agree about where the family meeting should take place. The best place is probably one that is quiet and away from small children. Your home is a good place, since that is where you keep your records in case any question comes up. Your home is also a physical reminder that these are the assets that you've worked for and that you are the one who is making the decisions.

Consult with your lawyer and possibly your accountant before you call the meeting. They can tell you if your proposed will complies with the laws of your state, if your plan takes advantage of available tax deductions, and if you need to make any other arrangements.

Not all decisions have to be made on the spot. Some families might prefer to spread the discussion out over several sessions. If there are complicated choices that need more study or emotional issues to be resolved, it may require some time for everyone to think through their options and choices.

The Question Of Equality

Should you divide your estate equally among your children? Many parents wrestle with this question. Even in the best of families there are rivalries. There may be clear reasons for dividing assets unequally—one child may have a physical or mental disadvantage, for example. Otherwise, you'll need to find your own balance among potentially conflicting considerations. You'll want to be comfortable with your arrangements, but do look at the larger picture as well. Your will can do harm; you can hurt feelings or set your children against one another. And don't forget the law of unintended consequences. Even when one child understands and accepts an inequality, there could be a resurgence of a childhood hangover: *you loved him more than you loved me!*

Why might some parents decide to treat children differently? Julia C. Spring, an associate clinical professor at Columbia University School of Law, says the "dynamics of the family" affect our planning. Someone in the family may be perceived as the good guy while someone else is suspected of having ulterior motives. Be careful, though; these perceptions may not be accurate.

Sometimes there are facts, not perceptions. Dan Edwards took one of his three sons into the family business. The son learned the business too well. He formed a rival business, using the customers he stole from his parents as his base. His brothers cut off all ties with him and urged their parents to cut him out of their will. They found this an understandable request but a difficult decision.

Sometimes grandchildren are good reasons for inequality. Louis and Doreen Brand thought, correctly as it turned out, that their son Lou, Jr. would not make good use of an inheritance. He lived up to and beyond his last penny. He never saved for his children's education, always assuming that "my parents will come through when my children need college tuition." Doreen outlived Louis, and when she died she gave her son and her daughter $10,000 bequests. The remainder of the estate was divided into equal inheritances for Lou's three children, with their aunt as the trustee. Their college tuition is now guaranteed.

Who Should Benefit?

There are times when parents agree that one child should receive more but fear repercussions from the other children. Perhaps the child who did more, took more responsibility, paid the bills, took a parent to doctor's appointments, or visited the parent in the hospital should be rewarded. But how do you do this?

One estate planner, without recommending the practice, suggests that you do this by giving privately and passing the property outside the will. You can name a child the joint owner of a property or an asset so that when you die, the child automatically inherits the property. You can open a bank account in trust for the child. You can name the child the beneficiary of a life insurance policy, United States Savings Bonds, or a retirement plan. You can set up a trust for the child, with you as trustee during your lifetime.

These arrangements are all legal (but check with a lawyer just the same). In each case, the asset will go to the chosen child after your death. In theory, your other children will never know. But don't count on keeping things secret. News about money travels and shows up in unexpected and unforeseen ways. It is like a leaky roof. There are no obvious cracks, but there are hidden passageways, and sooner or later the water trickles down and leaves a spot on the ceiling. In the same way a chance remark, an overheard conversation, a gossipy indiscretion all can undo your plans. Then your family has to pay the consequences. Family harmony can suffer.

Perhaps your children are not equally well off. Perhaps one was born smarter or married better. Perhaps one was lucky and picked a hotter career. Perhaps one learned to repair his car while his sister was collecting traffic tickets in her-not-yet-paid-off Mercedes? Should these children be treated equally?

Perhaps not, but the consensus remains that a will should treat every child equally, particularly because no one can say how the situation might change. What seems unequal today may not be tomorrow. Incomes and situations change, people lose jobs, illnesses strike. And there is a personal reason as well—we parents sometimes sit in judgment on our children's lifestyles without knowing all the facts. Our inheritance decisions can unintentionally chisel our misjudgments in stone.

One way to get around the problem of inequality is to emphasize family responsibility so that the better-off siblings look out for those who need help. If your family togetherness needs to be strengthened, now is the time to get started, which is yet another advantage of having this discussion early.

Explanations Are Necessary

If you decide to give more to one child than another, you need to explain your reasons. If possible, do this during the family meeting. Most children respond to fairness and are not going to worry about strict, dollar-for-dollar equality. But giving your explanations is important. Your kids need to understand that you are not showing favoritism but trying to enhance the future of each of them. If you're not comfortable explaining your reasons in person, then consider one estate lawyer's advice: leave your children a letter assuring them of your love and explaining why you have chosen to leave one child more than the others.

However you may arrange to settle your estate, your children should know your plans, whether they are equal or not. They should especially know if you are not distributing your estate equally and the reasons for your decision. If nothing else, this will help avoid hurt feelings, resentment, and bitterness. Where antagonism exists, the bitterness can lead to a legal challenge to the will. Permanent estrangement can result, no matter how the estate is finally settled.

Other Will Considerations

There are some other important factors that you need to consider during your estate planning. Should you leave your money to your children and their spouses, or just to your children? In this day of frequent divorce, bloodline should count. I recommend that you leave it—or the bulk of it, at any rate—to your children alone. Let them provide for their spouses. If you're concerned about your grandchildren, write them into your will separately.

Should your children's spouses be included in your family meetings? Only you can make this decision based on factors like your relationship with them, your evaluation of how they will react to the inheritance, and their relationship with the other spouses. There is no point in inviting sons-in-law or daughters-in-law who dislike each other. They will learn what they need to know from their own spouses anyway.

Who should be executor of your estate? Professor Spring thinks that this too can and should be discussed and decided at the family meetings. Whomever you choose should have some business and/or money management experience to handle the work prudently and competently. The person asked should have the time to do the work and be willing to undertake this major responsibility.

The choice of executor doesn't necessarily have to be made by parents—the children may decide among themselves who should take it on. This may actually be a better way to proceed, simply because it allows the kids to participate in the decision and gives them a choice and the right to consent instead of having the decision thrust upon them.

When you've taken care of all these questions you may sleep easier at night. And you might find it just a little easier to get through the pearly gates.

CHAPTER XXIII

We Are The New Pioneers

We don't travel in covered wagons and we don't cross oceans to a new land, but we're pioneers just the same. We share goals with those hardy souls who settle the New World from faraway lands. We too want peaceful, productive lives for our families; we'll challenge anyone who threatens them. And we have no objections to a little prosperity along the way.

The New World we are exploring is the inter-generational one. We owe our lavish gratitude to all the pioneers in science and medicine whose research and discoveries have extended our lives and allowed us to get here in the first place. We don't regret all those hours swimming laps, sweating in the gym, and running along the trail. Nor do we regret the times we nobly passed up the chocolates cake, the ice cream, and the frozen Margaritas (or the all times we didn't pass them up). All of it paid off.

Now we're among the first generations who can look forward to spending fifty or more years with our adult children and twenty or more years with our grandchildren. We may even get to play house or have a game of catch with our great-grandchildren! What a terrain to explore! We are a new phenomenon, drawing family road maps that others, especially our own children, will consult and maybe even follow.

Myths About Aging

Some aspects of our relationship are timeless. After all, the parent-child connection has been around since the first cave-father ran out of the cave to pull Dick and Jane out of the path of a roving lion and the first cave-mother fed them some raw lion meat. Parent-child relationships have always been based on love, dependence, and care.

Other aspects of our relationship have changed, some of them a lot, and those who study families haven't caught up yet. It's not unusual for students of cultural change to lag behind those who are living the changes. So myths about parents and parents of adults persist—*we are getting older, which means we must be becoming frail, isolated, and dependent.* In reality, we are healthy, independent, and living busy lives (with a few aches and pains perhaps, but nothing's perfect).

Interest in the elderly (whoever they are) has mush-roomed in the last few years. An entire field of study, Gerontology, is devoted to the study of the aging. It stands to reason. The population is getting older, so it's natural that professionals in the social work field would turn their attention to the problems of the elderly. Alas, the almost exclusive emphasis here is on *problems*. (Cynics say it's problems that are studied because it's problems that get funded.) One researcher noted that, at a recent World Congress on Gerontology, the people attending could have spent the entire Congress listening to papers on Alzheimer's disease and senile dementia. But those looking for session discussing older people as valuable resources for society would have had a lot of free time.

Bad news is always more dramatic than good news, so it's the bad news about families that gets the publicity. There are several very upsetting myths that, unfortunately, have been widely accepted. The first is that children dump their aging parents into nursing homes. It's simply not true. What is true is that families care for their older members with severe, chronic, degenerative diseases for as long as they can. Only when physical requirements and the need for round-the-clock attention or special medical facilities exceed the ability of most families do they place their parents in nursing homes.

Part of the misinformation comes from the fact that as people get older they do get sick. Sometimes they're in nursing homes until they recover and then return home. Many people enter nursing homes voluntarily because they have never been married or they have no family to care for them. More women than men are in nursing homes, since women outlive men by about seven years. But government statistics show that even among the very old (aged eighty-five and older), the vast majority—about seventy-five percent of women and eighty-five percent of men—do *not* live in nursing homes.

Is it true that older folks are dependent and unable to take care of themselves? Many older parents actually prefer to live alone, feeling secure with the knowledge that, in this day of cars and planes, they can reach their children, and vice versa, relatively quickly if they have to. One survey showed, in fact, that parents think it's more important to move near a doctor's office and a supermarket than near their children. (After all, unlike doctors, children make house calls and pick up groceries on the way.)

And all kinds of devices make it possible for people to live independently: special cutlery, long handled reachers, phones and clocks with large numbers, electronic devices that lock doors, and transmitters that call for help. Clap your hands and turn out the lights! (For my 85th birthday—but not before—I want a child's bright red Wristband Walkie Talkie so I can ask my husband to turn the kettle off while I'm tending my plants. Why should children have all the fun?) Most of these devices are easily within the budget of middle-income families.

Another myth is that parents and children don't have much contact. In point of fact, most older parents live close to family and are in frequent touch by phone and visit. We actually have more years together as a family, enjoying all that family life has come to mean.

This doesn't mean we get out of bed in the morning and say, "Wow, we're happy because we know we have a family that provides what sociology calls social support." We probably couldn't even define 'social support.' But sociologists can. They measure it by asking questions like, "How often does your relationship with your children make you feel 'loved and cared for," and "How much are your children willing to listen when you need to talk about your worries or problems?" At a very simple level, that's what social support is: having people who make us feel loved and cared for. It is so simple, and so profound. And it is not something that just disappears when we get older.

Has the Millennium Arrived?

Are we all warmly connected along the way? Of course not. We know our own challenges and we've listened to and sympathized with the troubles of our friends. Debra Umberson, a sociologist at the University of Texas, gives formal definition to what we have come to know intuitively: "the social connection with one's child or parent is [not] an unequivocal blessing for either generation. Social integration is double-edged. Close relationships are characterized by constraints and strains as well as rewards."

Of course we have dual roles; we are parents and grandparents. There is also a lot of confusion about who we are, simply because there is no such thing as *a* parent or *a* grandparent. Certainly, the advertisers who are trying to reach us are confused. They would like us to fit into neat little pigeon holes so they would know just what to say to make us buy their products. We persist in being individuals with a wide range of tastes and interests. They haven't decided what makes us 'mature' and therefore ready for their message. They complain that "brand loyalty does not increase with age" and that television shows "skewed to the 35 to 54-year-old-audience" were also attracting the 18–49 viewers. And vice versa. (Anyone for MTV?)

Our grandchildren can also be confused. An informal survey of my own concluded that grandchildren's expectations about their grandparents were shaped by story books and television. My granddaughter Laura summed it up for many when she said that as a child she pictured a grandmother as an "indulgent but frail old woman who lived in a cottage surrounded by flowers and baked cookies." Grandfathers were "indulgent old men, but not as indulgent as grandmothers, with white mustaches who took their grandchildren fishing." Most grandparents these days would only own up to the indulgent part.

Yes, some of us grandmothers still bake cookies, sew Hallowe'en costumes, stay with our daughters when they give birth, and sometimes babysit while they pursue their careers. Most of us love it. Others feel guilty because we don't have the time to do some of these things because we're too busy with our own careers. Some grandfathers do take their grandsons and their granddaughters fishing. Others stay in touch via E-mail. Some of us are lucky and live near our children and grandchildren; many of us have to settle for long visits and vacations together.

All of us have lived through so many changes in the family that a 1950's movie about the family would probably seem terribly anachronistic and quaint. As parents and grandparents we've learned to adjust to so much—cohabitation, boomerang kids, divorces, stepparenting, single mothers, unexpectedly unemployed fathers, adolescents who are ashamed to admit that they're still virgins. We sympathize with our children who worry in ways we never did about raising their children.

Some of their adjustments have been major. We never had to worry about things like serious crime in the schools or drug addiction among teenagers. They've made minor adjustments too. 'Pot' is not necessarily what you cook in; having guests for dinner has been complicated by things like salt-free, meat-free, and cholesterol-free diets: 'gross' is how you describe something 'yukky,' not your income before taxes.

Parents Emeriti

Are grandparents becoming an endangered species? Definitely not. Dr. Gunhild O. Hagestad notes that grandparents are "important supports for their children's parenting" and "important stabilizing forces" even for adult grandchildren. A grandparent, Hagestad points out, is "a family member who has lived and learned to put things in perspective, whose most important function may be just being there for younger generations."

Hagestad wonders when society will recognize that, as the population ages, more and more older people will "constitute a vastly underutilized social resource?" And when, she asks, will it be "understood that an aging society offers expanding, not constricting, opportunities for family life?"

Hagestad raises good questions. Happily, many of us could tell her how to answer them. As parents and grandparents we can never tell how much we influence our families. But we know we do. Nor can we tell how much our children have meant in our lives. But we know that we could never begin to measure it.

We should have no hesitation about the role we play in our children's lives and the role they play in ours. If we compare our lives to one stream and our children's lives to another, we can say both are deeper and stronger when they flow together. We have passed the boulders, the whitewater, the hairpin turns. We have enriched each other with each mile we have flowed together. And we continue to enrich each other as our lives flow through new and unexplored territory.

Yes, we are pioneers, but not everything in the world is new. We are parents and grandparents, and everything that has come to mean. We are continuity; we are ties to the traditions that have been passed from generation to generation and made the family so much more than a mere collection of related people. And we are the future. Where we have gone, our offspring are bound to go. Our children and grandchildren may not be able to appreciate who we are until they are standing where we stand now. When they embrace their children and grandchildren, they will finally know what we hope they have always know.

We love them.

Other
Resources

Aquilino, William S. *Unlaunched Adult Children and Parental Well-Being.* National Survey of Families and Household, Report No. 28.. Madison, Wisconsin: Center for Demography and Ecology, March 1990.

"An Exchange on Children and Divorce" (including Katherine R. Allen, "The Dispassionate Discourse of Children's Adjustment To Divorce"; Paul R. Amato, "Children's Adjustment to Divorce" and "Theories, Hypotheses, and Empirical Support: Family Structure, Family Process, and Family Ideology"; David H. Demo, "The Relentless Search for Effects of Divorce: Forging New Trails or Tumbling down the Beaten Path"; and Lawrence A. Kurdek, "Issues in Proposing a General Model of the Effects of Divorce on Children"). *Journal of Marriage and the Family,* February 1993, 23-54.

Asinof, Lynn. Handling an Estate without Inheriting Trouble." *Wall Street Journal,* July 15, 1994.

Auerbach, Sylvia. "Stepping Into Grandparenting." *Psychology Today,* April 1983, 56-57; "Changing Strides In Your 40's And 50's," *Sylvia Porter's Money Magazine,* April, 1985, 44-46; "Making Big Decisions About Money Should Be A Family Affair," *Physicians Financial News,* March 1985, 8-9; "A Cure For Money Fights," *New Woman,* October 1992, 134-35.

Bernard, Jessie. "The Good Provider Role, Its Rise And Fall." *American Psychologist,* January 1981, 1-12.

Brody, Jane. "Easing the Impact of a Divorce on Children." *New York Times,* July 24, 1991.

"Changing American Household." *American Demographics,* Supplement, July 1992, 1-25.

"Child Custody" (including Douglas B. Downey and Brian Powell, "Do Children in Single-Parent Households Fare Better Living with Same-Sex Parents"; and Daniel R. Meyer and Steven Garasky, "An Exchange on Children and Divorce"). *Journal of Marriage and the Family*, February 1993, 55-89.

Clemens, Audra W. and Leland J. Axelson. "The Not-So-Empty Nest: The Return of the Fledgling Adults." *Journal of Family Relations,* April 1985, 259-65.

Cowan, Alison Leigh. "Parenthood II: The Nest Won't Stay Empty." *New York Times*, March 12, 1989.

Dichter, Ernest. *Motivating Human Behavior*. New York: McGraw Hill, 1971.

Driscoll, Dave and Jo. *The Four "P's" for Stepparents*. Atlanta: Stepparent Association of America, Atlanta Metro Chapter, 1993.

Fisher, Barbara L., Paul R. Giblin, and Margaret H. Hoopes. "Healthy Family Functioning: What Therapists Say and What Families Want." *Journal of Marriage and Family Therapy*, July 1982, 273-84.

Flodin, Kim C. "Make Peace With Your Parents." *New Woman*, February 1992, 72-75.

Franks, Lucinda. "Little Big People." *New York Times Magazine*, October 20, 1993, 28-33.

Fried, Stephen and Carol Saline. "Grow Up Already! Lay Off Already! An Argument in Two Parts." *Philadelphia Magazine*, March 1989, 100-05, 165-75.

Furstenberg, Frank F. Jr. "Divorce and the American Family." *Annual Review, Sociology*, 1990, 379-403.

Gibson, Campbell. "The Four Baby Boomers." *American Demographics*, November 1993, 36-41.

Glazer, Sarah. "Affordable Housing: Is There Enough?." *Editorial Research Reports*, January 6, 1989, 2-12.

Glick, Paul C and Sung-Lin Lin. "More Single Young Adults Are Living With Their Parents: Who Are They?" *Journal of Marriage and the Family*, February 1986, 107-12.

Gross, Jane. "More Young Men Hang On To Apron Strings." *New York Times*, June 16, 1991.

Hanna, Sharon. "The Key To Successful Stepfamily Relationships." *Stepfamilies Quarterly*, Fall 1992, Winter 1992, Spring 1993.

Hokenson, Richard F. "Demographics, Profiles of a Changing Society." (Report). New York: Donaldson, Lufkin & Jenrette, 1990.

"Household and Family Characteristics." *Current Population Reports*. Washington, D.C.: Bureau of the Census, Economics and Statistics Administration, March 1991.

"Jobs." *Buisness Week*, February 22, 1993, 68-71.

Judis, John. "Jobless Recovery." *New Republic*, March 15, 1992, 20-23.

Krantzler, Mel. *Creative Divorce: A New Opportunity For Personal Growth.* New York: Signet, 1975.

Larson, Jan. "Understanding Stepfamilies." *American Demographics,* July 1992, 36-40.

Laurence, Leslie. "A Debt in the Family." *New Choices,* July 1990, 78-80.

Leimberg, Stephan R. Esq. and Charles K. Plotnick, Esq. "Financial Firedrill—What To Do Until the Lawyer Comes." (Brochure). Bryn Mawr, Pennsylvania: Financial Data Center.

Levin, Irene and Jan Trost. "Understanding the Concept of Family." *Journal of Family Relations,* July 1992, 348-51.

Lewen, Tamar. "Low Pay and Closed Doors Greet Young in Job Market." *New York Times*, March 10, 1994.

Longino, Charles F. Jr. "Myths Of An Aging America." *American Demographics,* August 1994, 36-42.

Lopez, Julie Amparano. "College Class of '93 Learns Hard Lesson: Career Prospects Are Worst in Decades." *Wall Street Journal,* May 5, 1993.

Lunder, Francesca Z. "Small Gadgets That Can Change Lives." *U.S. News & World Report*, March 6, 1989, 58-60.

Margulies, Sam. *Getting Divorced Without Ruining Your Life.* New York: Fireside, 1992.

McCollum, Eric E. "Mom, Dad...I Need Help." *New Choices,* May 1991, 85-86.

Mergenbagen, Paula. "Rethinking Retirement." *American Demographics,* June 1994. 28-34.

Millman, Marcia. *Warm Hearts and Cold Cash: The Intimate Dynamics of Families and Money.* New York: The Free Press, 1991.

Mitchell, Susan. "How To Talk To Young Adults." *American Demographics*, April 1993, 50-54.

Okimoto, Jean Davies and Phyllis Jackson Stegall. *Boomerang Kids: How To Live With Adult Children Who Return Home.* New York: Pocket Books, 1989.

National Survey on Communicating Family Values. Springfield, Maine: Massachusetts Mutual Insurance Company, December 1992.

Osterkamp, Lynn. *How To Deal with Your Parents When They Still Treat You Like a Child.* New York: Berkeley Books, 1992.

Pasley, Kay, David C. Dollahite, and Marilyn Ihinger-Tallman. "Bridging the Gap: Clinical Applications of Research Findings on the Spouse and Stepparent Roles in Remarriage." *Family Relations,* July 1993, 315-21.

Riche, Martha Farnsworth. "The Boomerang Age." *American Demographics*, May 1990, 24-30, 52.

Rigson, Joan E. "Student Loans Weigh Down Graduates." *Wall Street Journal*, January 3, 1991.

Rogers, Carl R. and F. J. Roethlisberger. "Barriers and Gateways to Communication." In *Fifteen Concepts for Managerial Success*. Cambridge: Harvard Business Review Business Classics, 1991.

Rossi, Alice S. and Peter H. *Of Human Bonding*. Hawthorne, New York: Aldine de Gruyter, 1990.

Rubenstein, Carin. "Money And Self-Esteem, Relationships, Secrecy, Envy, Satisfaction." *Psychology Today* Survey Report, 1981.

Schnaiberg, Allan and Sheldon Goldenberg. "From Empty Nest to Crowded Nest: The Dynamics of Incompletely Launched Young Adults." *Social Problems*, June 1989, 251-66.

Seltzer, Judith A. "Relationships between Fathers and Children Who Live Apart: The Father's Role after Separation." *Journal of Marriage and the Family,* February 1991, 70-71.

Arlene Skolnick. *Embattled Paradise: The American Family in an Age of Uncertainty*. New York: Basic Books, 1991.

"Status Report On The American Dream." *Changing Times*, March 1990, 41-50.

Stepfamilies Quarterly. Stepfamily Association of America, Inc., Lincoln, Nebraska.

Stepping Ahead Program. Lincoln, Nebraska: Stepfamily Association of America, 1988).

Tannen, Deborah. *You Just Don't Understand*. New York: Ballantine, 1990.

Tavris, Carol. *Anger: The Misunderstood Emotion*. Revised Edition. New York: Touchstone, 1989.

Uchitelle, Louis. "U.S. Wages. Not Getting Ahead? Better Get Used To It." *New York Times*, December 16, 1990.

Wallerstein, Judith S. with Sandra Blakeslee. *Second Chances: Men, Women, and Children a Decade after Divorce*. New York: Ticknor & Fields, 1989.

Welty, Ellen. "Money From Home—Can You Afford It?" *Mademoiselle*, May 1990, 148.

White, Jane. "Bouncing Back From Bad Credit." *Working Woman*, February 2, 1991.

Other Books From Silvercat Publications

✓ *Moving: A Complete Checklist and Guide for Relocation,* by Karen G. Adams (ISBN 0-9624945-6-9, $8.95). *Checklists, tips, and ideas from a veteran of 29 moves.*

✓ *The Travel Health Clinic Pocket Guide To Healthy Travel,* by Lawrence Bryson, M.D. (ISBN 0-9624945-4-2, $13.95). *Guidelines for traveling safely and staying healthy on the road by the Medical Director of San Francisco's* Travel Health Clinic.

✓ *The Country Club: Why Switching from the Big City to the Boondocks Could Be Your Smartest Move Ever,* by Dale Wildman (ISBN 0-9624945-5-0, $8.95). *Practical tips and frank, useful advice and encouragement about moving to the country from someone who did it.*

✓ *A Quick Guide To Food Safety,* by Robert L. Goodman (ISBN 0-9624945-3-4, $6.95). *Suggestions and guidelines for a safe and healthy diet.*

Order form

Title	#	Each	Amount
			$_____
			_____
			_____
		Subtotal	$_____
California residents, please add 7% sales tax			_____
		Total	$_____

❑ Please add me to your mailing list.

Payment method:
  ❑ Check or money order enclosed.
  ❑ Please charge my credit card: ❑ VISA   ❑ MasterCard
  Account # _____ Exp. date _____
  Name on card_____
  Daytime phone_____
  Signature_____

Send to:
  Name _____
  Address _____
  _____
  City _____ State, zip _____

Order from: Silvercat Publications
4070 Goldfinch St., Ste. C
San Diego, CA 92103-1865
(619) 299-6774 / (619) 299-9119 fax